CONQUERING BURNOUT

An Individualized Approach for Reducing Stress,
Nurturing Personal Relationships, and Improving Your
Overall Health & Wellness

M.L. WINTERS

Table of Contents

Introduction

Every year, millions of people find themselves whispering, "I can't keep going like this," as they struggle under the weight of burnout. It's a silent epidemic, affecting people from all walks of life—teachers, parents, artists, workers—leaving a trail of exhaustion and disconnection in its wake. Yet, despite its prevalence, the path to recovery often remains shrouded in mystery and misconception.

My name and passion may be new to you, but my dedication to mental wellness is deeply rooted in my professional life as a certified mental health and addictions worker and my academic background with an associate degree in psychology. Through my years of study and firsthand experiences with clients, I have come to recognize the profound impact of burnout on individuals' productivity and overall quality of life.

This book is born out of a desire to break down the complexities of burnout into manageable, relatable pieces. It is crafted to be an accessible guide that offers practical advice grounded in professional knowledge but enriched with real-world applicability. Each chapter is designed to walk you through understanding your own experiences with burnout, armed with strategies that cater to diverse lifestyles and challenges.

This book empathizes with your struggles, supports your journey, and inspires you to implement changes that can significantly enhance your well-being. We will explore the symptoms and causes of burnout and the deeply personal stories of those who have walked this path before you. This blend of professional insight and personal narrative aims to provide a holistic view of effectively managing and overcoming the stressors that lead to burnout.

What sets this book apart is its commitment to an individualized approach. Unlike one-size-fits-all solutions, it acknowledges the unique circumstances of each person's life, offering a variety of perspectives and tools that can be tailored to your specific needs and situations.

As we proceed, expect to find yourself reflected in the pages of this book, see your challenges being addressed, and discover new ways to nurture your personal relationships and improve your health and wellness.

Are you ready to step out of the shadow of burnout and rediscover the vibrancy of a life well-lived? Let's begin this journey together, equipped with knowledge, empowered by understanding, and inspired by the possibility of renewal.

ONE

Understanding Burnout

In today's fast-paced society, burnout has emerged as a silent epidemic, a condition that discreetly erodes the energy and enthusiasm of countless individuals. As you navigate your daily responsibilities, you might find yourself in a state where the tasks that once sparked joy now evoke a sense of dread. This chapter aims to unpack the layers of burnout, helping you understand its roots and recognize its pervasive symptoms. By arming yourself with knowledge, you can begin to take proactive steps toward reclaiming your energy and zest for life.

1.1 Defining Burnout: More Than Just Stress

To grasp the full scope of burnout, it's crucial to differentiate it from its close relative: stress. While stress is almost a badge of honor in our productivity-driven lives, acting as a motivator to push you to meet deadlines and tackle challenges, burnout is its shadowy counterpart. Burnout doesn't propel you forward; it breaks you down. It is a state of emotional, physical, and mental exhaustion brought on by prolonged exposure to demanding situations. Unlike ordinary stress, which can be managed and often dissipates after the situation is resolved, burnout leaves you feeling empty, incapable of coping, and devoid of energy.

At the core of burnout are three primary symptoms: overwhelming exhaustion, feelings of cynicism and detachment from the job, and a sense of ineffectiveness and lack of accomplishment. When you're burned out, waking up each morning feels like a monumental task. You may feel disconnected from your job or colleagues, negatively viewing your work environment. Projects or relationships that once motivated you might now seem pointless. This detachment is not just a bad day at the office; it is a deep-rooted disillusionment that can significantly hinder your ability to function effectively at work and at home.

The consequences of ignoring symptoms of burnout can be severe, affecting all dimensions of your health and life. Physically, the constant state of stress can lead to debilitating conditions such as hypertension, chronic fatigue, and immune disorders. Mentally, it can manifest as depression and anxiety, clouding your ability to think clearly and make sound decisions. Professionally, burnout often results in decreased productivity and a high rate of absenteeism, which can jeopardize your career.

Consider the story of Michael, a senior software developer who loved his job coding and solving complex problems. Over time, however, the relentless deadlines and overwhelming workload began to take a toll. Michael started working longer hours, sacrificing sleep and personal time.

Despite his dedication to his job, he felt that he was never catching up. His initial enthusiasm for his job waned, replaced by a perpetual sense of exhaustion and frustration. He became irritable and detached from his co-workers, and his performance suffered. This real-world example underscores the importance of recognizing the early signs of burnout and acting before it escalates into a crisis.

Understanding burnout is the first step toward healing. Keep Michael's story in mind as we move forward in this chapter. It is a testament to the fact that while burnout can be debilitating, recognizing and addressing it promptly can put you on the path to recovery and prevent severe consequences. This chapter aims to guide you through the intricacies of this condition, offering insights and practical strategies to revive your enthusiasm and regain control over your professional and personal life. As you read on, remember that recognizing the problem is the beginning of your path to recovery.

1.2 The Physiology of Burnout: What Happens in Your Body

When we begin to peel back the layers of burnout, it becomes evident that it's not solely a psychological or emotional issue; it's deeply physiological. The sustained stress that leads to burnout triggers a cascade of hormonal reactions within your body, fundamentally altering your physical state. Central to this process are cortisol and adrenaline, hormones that your body releases during stress. These are part of your body's fight-or-flight response, initially designed to protect you in moments of acute danger. However, in the modern context of continuous stress, their prolonged presence in your system can lead to significant health issues.

Cortisol, often called the "stress hormone," regulates various functions in your body, including metabolism and immune response. Under stress, elevated cortisol levels can temporarily boost energy and immunity. However, when stress becomes chronic, high cortisol levels can lead to serious health problems such as weight gain, hypertension, and a weakened immune system, making you more susceptible to infections and diseases. Adrenaline, which increases your heart rate and elevates your blood pressure and energy supplies, can lead to cardiovascular damage if these levels remain elevated over a long period.

The physical symptoms associated with these hormonal changes are varied but significantly impactful. Many people experiencing burnout report chronic headaches and muscle tension, often attributed to elevated cortisol levels. Gastrointestinal issues such as irritable bowel syndrome can also manifest as stress alters the gut microbiota and increases gut permeability. Furthermore, disrupted sleep patterns are a hallmark of burnout; high cortisol levels can disrupt the natural circadian rhythms, leading to insomnia or sleep that is not refreshing, which only exacerbates fatigue and decreases resilience to stress.

Beyond these physical symptoms, burnout can profoundly affect brain function. Chronic stress impacts areas of the brain responsible for memory, concentration, and emotional regulation. The hippocampus, vital for learning and memory, can become less effective under constant stress, leading to memory lapses and difficulty concentrating. Moreover, the amygdala, which processes emotions, can become overactive, making you more receptive to negative stimuli and thus more prone to feelings of anxiety and depression. These neurological changes affect your professional performance and how you interact with others, potentially straining personal and professional relationships.

Preventive measures and lifestyle changes are crucial in mitigating these physiological effects. Regular physical activity can be remarkably effective, as exercise reduces cortisol levels and stimulates the production of endorphins, chemicals in the brain that act as natural painkillers and mood elevators. Additionally, a balanced diet rich in antioxidants, omega-3 fatty acids, and fiber can support brain health and reduce inflammation, countering some of the negative effects of stress hormones. Prioritizing sleep is also essential; establishing a regular sleep schedule and creating a restful sleeping environment can help realign your body's natural circadian rhythms. Lastly, incorporating relaxation techniques such as deep breathing exercises, yoga, or meditation into your daily routine can significantly reduce the production of stress hormones and boost your overall resilience to stress.

Understanding the intricate dance of hormones and physiological responses that comprise the burnout experience illuminates why it feels so overwhelming and why it's so challenging to overcome. It underscores the necessity of a holistic approach to prevention and recovery, including strategic lifestyle adjustments to rebalance your physical and mental health. As we explore the full spectrum of burnout, the importance of addressing its psychological aspects and physiological roots becomes increasingly clear, providing a more comprehensive framework for effective intervention and recovery.

1.3 Psychological Triggers of Burnout: The Mind-Body Connection

Burnout does not occur in isolation; it is a multidimensional phenomenon where psychological factors play a crucial role. Understanding these triggers is key to developing strategies that address and mitigate burnout before it takes a firm hold. One of the most prevalent psychological triggers is the perceived lack of control over one's work environment and outputs. When you feel that you have little to no control over your work tasks or outcomes, stress levels can skyrocket, leaving you feeling helpless and overwhelmed. Unclear job expectations can exacerbate this perceived loss of control. Without clear guidelines or objectives, you may find yourself floundering, unsure if your efforts align with what is expected, leading to increased anxiety and stress.

Dysfunctional workplace dynamics also significantly contribute to burnout. Environments where communication is poor, support is lacking, and conflict is frequent create a breeding ground for stress. Additionally, extremes of activity —whether monotony or chaos—disrupt your ability to find a rhythm at work, making it hard to maintain engagement and motivation. Monotony can lead to boredom and a sense of stagnation, while chaos can cause anxiety and prevent you from completing tasks effectively due to constant interruptions or changes in direction.

Another profound trigger is the misalignment between one's personal values and the job's demands or ethics. When there is a disconnect between what you value and what your job requires of you, it breeds discontent and can lead to moral injury, where you feel you are betraying your core values. This dissonance is particularly damaging as it attacks the very essence of who you are, leading to deep-seated dissatisfaction and increasing the risk of burnout.

Developing psychological resilience can be a powerful buffer against these triggers. Resilience allows you to adapt to adverse situations, handle stress more effectively, and quickly recover from setbacks. It involves maintaining flexibility and balance in your life as you face stressful circumstances and traumatic events. Building resilience is not about toughening up or going it alone; rather, it involves cultivating a strong support network, learning to manage your emotions, maintaining a positive outlook, and seeing challenges as opportunities for growth rather than insurmountable obstacles.

To manage stress at a psychological level effectively, begin by practicing mindfulness. This technique helps you stay present and engaged, providing a tool to manage stress by focusing your attention on the here and now rather than worrying about future uncertainties or ruminating over past mistakes. Additionally, setting realistic goals is crucial; they should be challenging enough to motivate you but achievable enough to prevent feelings of failure and frustration. Start by breaking larger objectives into smaller, manageable tasks and setting clear, measurable milestones. This approach provides a sense of control and creates opportunities for small victories, boosting your morale and resilience against burnout.

Incorporating these strategies into your daily routine can significantly alter your psychological response to stressors, providing a stronger foundation to handle the pressures that come with professional responsibilities. Remember, the goal is not to eliminate stress entirely—which is an unrealistic expectation—but to manage it in ways that preserve your health and well-being. By understanding the psychological triggers of burnout and implementing strategies to counteract them, you equip yourself with the tools necessary to maintain balance and prevent the deep-seated exhaustion that burnout can cause. This proactive approach allows you to enjoy a more fulfilling professional life and safeguards your mental health.

1.4 The Stages of Burnout: Recognizing Your Position

Understanding the progression of burnout is essential to managing and eventually overcoming it. Burnout does not appear suddenly; it develops in stages, each with its own set of challenges and symptoms. Recognizing which stage you are in can significantly enhance your ability to deal with burnout effectively and prevent its escalation. The journey typically moves from initial enthusiasm to stagnation, escalating to frustration and culminating in apathy. Each stage reflects a deeper level of emotional and physical depletion, and identifying these can serve as a crucial first step in your recovery process.

In the first stage, **enthusiasm**, you might find yourself taking on tasks with vigor and dedication. This is where your energy levels are high, and your commitment to work is strong. However, without adequate boundaries and rest, this can quickly lead to the second stage: **stagnation**. Here, you might begin to feel that no matter how hard you work, you're not achieving enough or that your continuous effort isn't yielding the results you expected. This feeling of running in place can be incredibly disheartening, leading to **frustration**, the third stage. During frustration, your initial enthusiasm turns into persistent dissatisfaction. Tasks that once seemed challenging in a positive way now feel insurmountable. The culmination of this path is **apathy**, a stage where you might feel emotionally numb or indifferent towards your work, experiencing a significant disconnect from your job and even your personal life.

Recognizing these stages in yourself can be challenging, but it is crucial for taking proactive steps towards recovery. To assist in this self-recognition, consider integrating self-assessment checklists into your routine. These can include reflective questions that help pinpoint feelings of disillusionment, fatigue, or detachment that are often ignored in the busyness of daily tasks. For instance, regularly ask yourself: Do I feel less enthusiastic about projects I once enjoyed? Do I often feel tired even after resting? Am I becoming cynical or detached from my colleagues? Answering these can help you identify early signs of burnout, allowing for timely interventions.

The significance of early detection and intervention cannot be overstated. By acknowledging the symptoms when they first appear, you can implement strategies to halt the progression of burnout. For example, if you are in the stagnation phase, it might be time to reassess your workload and set clearer boundaries. This could involve negotiating tasks with your supervisor or learning to say "no" to additional responsibilities you cannot manage. Each stage requires a tailored approach; what works during the enthusiasm stage (such as setting realistic goals to prevent overcommitment) might differ significantly from what is needed in the apathy stage (such as seeking professional help or taking a sabbatical to recharge).

Preventive tips are also stage specific. Proactively communicating about your workload and taking regular breaks can be effective in the early stages. As you move towards the frustration stage, techniques such as seeking support from peers or mentors and engaging in professional development to regain a sense of competence and accomplishment can be beneficial. More intensive strategies like therapy, long-term rest, or even career reassessment might become necessary in the latter stages.

It's important to remember that moving through these stages is not a sign of failure but a common experience for many professionals across various fields. By understanding and recognizing where you are in these stages, you can better navigate your responses and implement strategies that alleviate symptoms and contribute to a more fulfilling professional life. This approach not only aids in your recovery but also empowers you to handle future stressors more effectively, promoting a sustainable balance between your personal and professional life.

1.5 Burnout in Different Life Stages: From Millennials to Boomers

Burnout is not a selective phenomenon; it spans generations, each experiencing nuances influenced by distinct values, life stages, and the ever-evolving technological landscape. Millennials, Generation X, and Baby Boomers navigate through their career paths under varied economic climates and societal expectations, which mold their experiences of stress and burnout. Millennials might face unique challenges when stepping into their careers amidst the digital boom and economic uncertainty. Their work life is heavily integrated with technology, leading to phenomena like an 'always on' culture, which blurs the boundaries between work and personal life. This generation values flexibility and purpose in their careers, which, when unmet, can lead to dissatisfaction and burnout. Practical strategies for millennials might include establishing clear boundaries between work and personal time, advocating for telecommuting options, and finding roles that align closely with their values for a more fulfilling career path.

On the other hand, Generation X, often caught between the demands of raising a family and caring for aging parents, faces a different kind of stress. Known as the 'sandwich generation,' they manage multiple responsibilities, which can significantly strain their time and energy resources. For Gen Xers, effective strategies to manage burnout might involve seeking flexible work arrangements, setting priorities that allow for quality family time, and utilizing support networks for caregiving responsibilities. It's also beneficial for members of this generation to engage in regular self-care routines that help maintain their physical and mental health amidst their numerous obligations.

Baby Boomers, many of whom are nearing or have entered retirement, encounter burnout in forms that might not be immediately recognized. After years of defining themselves through their professions, the transition can be jarring, leading to feelings of uselessness or lack of purpose, which are classic precursors to burnout. For those still in the workforce, keeping up with rapid technological advancements can be a source of stress. Tailored advice for Baby Boomers includes developing a transition plan that gradually reduces work commitments while incorporating activities that provide a sense of purpose and joy. Additionally, staying current with technology through workshops or courses can reduce stress and increase engagement at work.

The integration of technology in the workplace presents varied challenges and benefits across these generations. Millennials are digital experts who are comfortable with technology, but they often face the downside of digital overload, where the lines between work and personal life blur, leading to burnout. In contrast, Baby Boomers might feel overwhelmed by the fast pace of technological advancement, which can contribute to a sense of alienation and stress at work. Therefore, effective management strategies must be generation-specific, recognizing each cohort's particular challenges. For instance, while younger workers may benefit from digital detox strategies and effective training on managing digital communication, older employees might appreciate supportive training that helps them navigate new technologies at their own pace.

Consider the example of a technology firm that implemented a tiered training program tailored to different comfort levels with digital tools. Younger employees were offered advanced courses on leveraging technology for efficient work management, while older employees received basic training that focused on mastering essential digital skills. This approach improved productivity and reduced feelings of inadequacy and stress, directly addressing the generational divide in technological adaptation.

Understanding these generational differences is crucial in developing effective strategies to manage and prevent burnout. Each stage of life brings different priorities and challenges, and recognizing this allows for a more empathetic and effective approach to fostering a healthy work environment. As we continue to explore the multifaceted nature of burnout, it becomes evident that tailored interventions that respect individual and generational experiences are key to maintaining productivity and a balanced and satisfying life.

1.6 Gender and Burnout: A Closer Look at How It Affects Men and Women Differently

Burnout, while universal, does not manifest uniformly across gender lines. Societal expectations and roles significantly influence how stress is experienced and managed, thereby affecting the susceptibility and response to burnout differently for men and women. Often stereotyped as the breadwinners and less likely to seek help, men may bottle up their stresses, leading to explosive manifestations of burnout. On the other hand, women frequently juggle multiple roles — professionals, mothers, and caretakers — and the relentless pursuit of perfection in each can lead to gradual yet profound emotional and physical exhaustion.

The workplace, a central arena where burnout unfolds, often mirrors and magnifies these gender-specific stressors. Despite strides towards equality, women frequently encounter systemic barriers such as wage disparity, under-representation in leadership roles, and inadequate support for work-life balance. Such disparities diminish professional growth opportunities and contribute significantly to stress and eventual burnout. Men, while generally facing fewer systemic barriers, often encounter cultural expectations to prioritize work over personal well-being, which can similarly lead to burnout. Moreover, traditional norms discouraging emotional expression can prevent men from seeking help or even acknowledging burnout, letting it silently progress.

Recent studies underscore these dynamics, revealing that women report higher levels of work-related stress compared to men, yet they are also more likely to seek and utilize coping resources. This discrepancy highlights the need for gender-specific strategies to effectively address and mitigate burnout. Creating environments that support professional advancement and personal obligations, such as flexible work arrangements or robust parental leave policies, can be crucial for women. Furthermore, initiatives that foster mentorship and leadership training can empower women and reduce feelings of isolation and stagnation at work.

Destigmatizing help-seeking behavior is equally important for men. Encouraging open conversations about mental health, stress, and burnout in male-dominated work environments can foster a more supportive atmosphere. Initiatives could include training sessions focused on building emotional intelligence and resilience and promoting work-life balance as a priority for all employees, regardless of gender. Providing access to anonymous mental health resources and ensuring that workplace policies do not inadvertently penalize time off for personal well-being are also vital steps in addressing burnout among men.

In terms of coping strategies, women may benefit from assertiveness training to better navigate workplace dynamics and effectively advocate for their needs and boundaries. Networking groups and support circles that connect women across various industries can also serve as excellent platforms for sharing strategies to manage stress and prevent burnout. For men, strategies might include promoting hobbies or physical activities that offer a healthy outlet for stress relief and provide opportunities for informal peer support. Encouraging men to engage in regular health check-ups and mental health screenings can also be crucial, as these practices help in the early identification and management of stress and burnout.

Recent research published in the *Journal of Occupational Health Psychology* supports these gender-specific approaches and highlights the effectiveness of tailored interventions in reducing burnout. For instance, programs that address specific stressors such as work-life conflict or job insecurity can significantly improve job satisfaction and overall well-being. This evidence supports the need for targeted strategies that acknowledge and address the unique ways in which men and women experience and cope with burnout.

Understanding these nuanced dynamics is not just about fostering a fairer workplace or society; it's about effectively combating burnout in a way that acknowledges and respects individual experiences. As we continue to explore and address these issues, it becomes clear that tailored, informed approaches are crucial for preventing burnout and promoting a healthier, more balanced professional life for everyone. Recognizing and adapting to these gender-specific needs and challenges is not just beneficial but necessary for creating sustainable work environments where all individuals can thrive without the risk of burnout.

TWO

Practical Recovery Strategies

Recovery from burnout is not a one-size-fits-all solution. It's a deeply personal journey that requires you to listen intently to your own needs and respond with strategies that respect your individual circumstances. In this chapter, we'll explore how to craft a recovery plan that addresses the universal elements of burnout and aligns seamlessly with your unique life situation. The goal here is not just to recover temporarily but rather to build a foundation strong enough to ward off future stressors.

2.1 Customizing Your Recovery: Plans That Fit Your Life

Every person's experience with burnout is shaped by a complex combination of individual factors, including work environment, personal life, and inherent stressors. Recognizing this, the first step in your recovery should be a careful assessment of your specific circumstances. Begin by considering what aspects of your life contribute most significantly to your stress. Is it the unrelenting deadlines at work? Perhaps the juggling act between professional responsibilities and family needs? Or even the chronic feeling of never being able to catch up? Understanding these triggers is crucial as it helps tailor a recovery plan that addresses your particular challenges.

Once you clearly understand your stressors, the next step is to develop personalized recovery strategies. This involves setting realistic, achievable goals aligned with your values and current life situation. For instance, if a significant part of your stress comes from a lack of time spent with family, one of your recovery goals might be to reorganize your schedule to incorporate more family time. Or, if constant connectivity is burning you out, setting boundaries around digital device usage could be a beneficial goal. The key here is to ensure these goals are about reducing stress and enhancing your overall life satisfaction.

Flexibility is another critical component of any effective recovery plan. As you implement different strategies, your circumstances and needs might change, necessitating adjustments to your plan. For instance, what works for you at the beginning of your recovery might not be as effective when you start feeling better and regaining more energy. Therefore, it's important to regularly review and adjust your recovery plan. This adaptability helps maintain the relevance of your plan and empowers you to take control of your recovery process, adjusting as needed to stay on track.

To illustrate the power of a personalized recovery plan, consider the story of Linda, a project manager in a busy tech company. Linda's burnout manifested itself through physical exhaustion and a sense of disillusionment with her career. Her recovery plan included specific, tailored strategies such as delegating non-essential tasks, scheduling regular check-ins with her team to improve communication, and setting aside time each week for professional development and personal reflection. Over time, these changes helped reduce her stress levels significantly, and she found herself more engaged and fulfilled in her work. Linda's story is a testament to how understanding one's unique needs and crafting a personalized plan can lead to successful recovery from burnout.

Interactive Element: Personalized Recovery Plan Worksheet

To help you start your own customized recovery journey, below is a worksheet designed to guide you through the process of assessing your stressors, setting relevant recovery goals, and planning flexible strategies. This tool aims to provide a structured approach to creating a recovery plan that resonates with your individual needs.

1. Assessment of Stressors: List the top three sources of stress in your current life.
2. Setting Recovery Goals: For each stressor listed above, set a specific, measurable, and achievable goal that addresses the underlying issue.
3. Strategies for Each Goal: List the strategies you plan to implement to achieve each goal.

4. Review Schedule: Decide how frequently you will review and adjust your recovery plan (e.g., once a month, every three months).

By taking the time to fill out this worksheet, you not only gain clarity on what needs to be addressed but also take the first step toward active recovery. Remember, the most effective recovery plan is one that you truly own—one that is crafted by you, for you.

2.2 Quick Wins: Small Changes for Immediate Relief

Sometimes, the smallest adjustments can lead to the most significant relief in the quest to overcome burnout. It's not always the grand gestures but rather the minute, everyday changes that accumulate to help reduce stress levels and enhance your daily life. Let's start with some simple yet effective relaxation techniques that you can incorporate immediately into your routine. Breathing exercises, for instance, are a powerful tool for immediate stress relief. Try the 4-7-8 breathing method: breathe in for 4 seconds, hold for 7 seconds, and exhale for 8 seconds. This technique helps regulate the heart rate and can instantly bring about a sense of calmness. Similarly, guided imagery, where you visualize a peaceful scene or setting, can significantly divert your mind from stressors, providing a quick mental getaway. Quick meditative practices, even if just for a few minutes a day, can reset your stress levels and enhance your focus and productivity.

Making small daily adjustments is another cornerstone of immediate stress relief. Consider the setup of your workspace—something as simple as adjusting the ergonomics can reduce physical strain and, by extension, lower stress. Ensure that your chair supports your back comfortably, your computer screen is at eye level, and your wrists are not strained while typing. Additionally, instituting regular short breaks throughout your workday can prevent the buildup of stress. Even a five-minute pause every hour to stand, stretch, or walk around can make a substantial difference in how you feel by the end of the day. Setting boundaries for work hours is also crucial; define a clear end to your workday where you step away from all work-related tasks, which helps prevent burnout by maintaining a healthy work-life balance.

Communication hacks can also offer instant relief by managing expectations with colleagues and superiors, which is often a significant source of stress. Clear and assertive communication can prevent misunderstandings and the accumulation of unspoken grievances, which can contribute to stress and burnout. Start by being clear about your capacity and realistic about your timelines. When new tasks are assigned, discuss openly how these fit with your current workload. Ask for priorities to be adjusted or for deadlines to be extended if necessary. This helps manage your stress and builds a culture of open communication and realistic expectation setting at your workplace.

Leveraging technology can provide quick support and accessible tools to manage your stress levels effectively. Numerous apps and online resources are available that can guide you through mindfulness exercises and stress management techniques and offer peer support. These resources can be particularly useful for those who may not have immediate access to professional help or those seeking to manage their stress independently. Apps like *Headspace* or *Calm* offer guided meditation sessions that can be done anywhere and anytime, fitting easily into a busy schedule. They also provide a platform to connect with others who are facing similar challenges, offering community support that can be incredibly reassuring.

By implementing these simple techniques and adjustments, you can start to see immediate improvements in your stress levels, potentially halting the progression of burnout. Remember, the goal is to integrate these small changes into your daily routine, so they become second nature, contributing to long-term stress management and overall well-being. The impact of these 'quick wins' is often under-estimated, yet they form an essential part of the foundation upon which more comprehensive recovery strategies can be built. As you continue to apply these simple strategies, observe the changes in how you feel and function, adjusting as needed to optimize the benefits and sustain your recovery from burnout.

2.3 Long-term Strategies for Sustained Recovery

Embarking on the path to long-term recovery from burnout requires immediate relief strategies while cultivating habits and routines that fortify your resilience and ensure sustained well-being. One effective method to instill lasting changes is through habit formation techniques such as habit stacking. This involves linking new, desirable habits to a sequence of existing ones, thereby creating a chain of habits that natu-rally flow from one to another. For instance, if your goal is to reduce stress through mindfulness, you might stack this new habit on top of your morning coffee routine—spending a few minutes meditating right after you enjoy your coffee each morning. This linkage helps solidify the new habit by associating it with an established one and also structures your day in a way that supports ongoing stress management.

Reminders can also be crucial in integrating new habits into your daily life. Whether through apps that send you notification prompts or physical notes placed strategically around your home or workspace, reminders can serve as cues to engage in behavior conducive to recovery and wellness. They keep your recovery goals at the forefront of your mind, helping to maintain focus and consistency in your efforts. Over time, these repeated actions become more automatic, reducing the mental effort required to carry them out and thus embedding them deeply into your routine.

Another fundamental aspect of long-term recovery is regularly reevaluating your routines and commitments. This reflective practice involves assessing how well your current habits and activities align with your recovery goals and making adjustments as needed. It's about asking yourself whether your commitments are nourishing or depleting your energy. Are they contributing to your sense of purpose and satisfaction, or are they sources of unnecessary stress? This ongoing appraisal helps eliminate or alter stress-inducing activities and ensures that your routines continue to evolve in ways that support your health and happiness.

Sustainable work-life integration is pivotal in preventing the recurrence of burnout. This doesn't necessarily mean splitting your time evenly between work and personal life; rather, it means finding a blend that allows you to thrive in both areas without feeling overwhelmed. Strategies here might include setting clear boundaries between work and personal time, such as having designated times when you are unavailable for work-related communications. It also involves recognizing the importance of downtime and ensuring that leisure activities are not an afterthought but a priority. Engaging regularly in activities that disconnect you from work-related thoughts allows your mind and body to recover, replenishing your energy for future tasks.

Developing resilience is crucial in fortifying yourself against the pressures that lead to burnout in the first place. Techniques such as cognitive reframing can transform your perception of stressful situations, allowing you to view them as challenges rather than insurmountable problems. This shift in perspective can significantly reduce the emotional impact of stressors, making them more manageable. Additionally, actively seeking meaning in your work and personal activities can enhance your engagement and satisfaction, acting as a buffer against stress. When your daily activities resonate with your personal values and goals, they become more fulfilling, which naturally diminishes the likelihood of burnout.

Through these strategies—habit formation, routine reevaluation, work-life integration, and resilience development—you create a robust framework for your life that addresses the symptoms of burnout and builds a resilient structure against future stress. This proactive approach ensures that your recovery is not just about getting back to where you were but moving forward to where you want to be, with greater control and fulfillment in your professional and personal life. As you implement these strategies, remember that the goal is continuous improvement and adaptation, allowing you to navigate life's challenges with strength and grace.

2.4 Integrating Professional Help: When to Seek It

Recognizing when to seek professional help is a pivotal step in your recovery from burnout. Many struggle with identifying the right moment or signs that indicate the need for professional intervention. Key indicators include persistent feelings of depression or anxiety that don't seem to improve despite your best efforts at self-care or implementing recovery strategies. If you find yourself in a constant state of mental exhaustion, experiencing intrusive thoughts that hinder your daily functionality, or facing emotional numbness where you once had passion, these are significant signs that professional help might be necessary. Similarly, if your relationships start to suffer or your work performance declines drastically due to stress and fatigue, it's crucial to consider seeking help from a mental health professional.

Finding the right professional is a process that requires careful consideration to ensure that the help you receive is tailored to your needs and effective in aiding your recovery. Start by looking for healthcare providers specializing in stress management, mental health issues related to occupational stress, or specifically in burnout recovery. Psychologists, licensed counselors, and wellness coaches can offer different perspectives and forms of therapy that might be beneficial. When choosing a professional, consider factors such as their credentials, areas of specialization, treatment approaches, and patient reviews. It's also important to consider the rapport you have with them; a therapist who makes you feel understood and safe can significantly enhance the effectiveness of the therapy.

Navigating mental health services can initially seem daunting, but understanding what to expect can ease this process. Typically, initial consultations involve discussing your stressors, symptoms, lifestyle, and previous mental health history. This helps the professional assess your situation and tailor a treatment plan that integrates seamlessly with your personal recovery efforts. Therapy might include cognitive-behavioral techniques to help reframe negative thoughts, sessions focused on developing coping strategies, or even group therapy to provide support from others who are dealing with similar issues. Integrating professional help into your recovery means viewing it as a complement to your ongoing efforts, such as maintaining healthy routines and implementing stress-reduction techniques discussed earlier in this book.

Lastly, it is essential to de-stigmatize seeking help for burnout and stress-related issues. Historically, there has been a reluctance to seek mental health services, often rooted in myths that it signifies weakness or a failure to handle one's problems independently. On the contrary, acknowledging the need for help and taking action to seek it is a profound strength and an important step in your recovery journey. It is a practical approach grounded in the understanding that just like physical illnesses, mental health issues benefit from professional expertise and intervention. By seeking help, you prioritize your well-being and take control of your life, demonstrating courage and practicality in managing your health.

By addressing these aspects—recognizing the need for help, finding the right professional, navigating mental health services, and overcoming stigma—you can significantly enhance your ability to recover from burnout. Professional help provides support and equips you with tools and strategies designed to offer relief and foster long-term resilience, enabling you to return to a life of productivity and meaning without the looming shadow of burnout.

2.5 The Role of Nutrition in Combating Burnout

The adage "you are what you eat" holds profound truth, especially when dealing with burnout. Your body's nutritional intake is crucial in handling stress, recovering from fatigue, and maintaining overall mental acuity. Integrating a balanced diet is not just about physical health—it's a fundamental part of mental wellness. When your body receives the right nutrients, it can produce energy more efficiently, stabilize mood, and enhance resilience against stress. Let's explore how you can utilize nutrition to fortify your body and mind against the pressures that lead to burnout.

The connection between food and mood is supported by numerous studies indicating that certain diets can boost energy and mitigate the effects of stress. For example, complex carbohydrates found in whole grains, fruits, and vegetables can increase serotonin levels in the brain, which has a calming effect. On the other hand, proteins from lean sources such as chicken, fish, beans, and nuts provide amino acids like tyrosine, which help enhance mental clarity and energy levels. Including these foods in your diet can help stabilize your energy throughout the day and reduce mood swings, thus helping you handle stress more effectively.

Moreover, specific nutrients play a significant role in modulating the body's stress response. Magnesium, for example, is known for its ability to relax muscles and reduce symptoms of fatigue—a common component of burnout. Foods rich in magnesium, such as spinach, almonds, and avocados, should be a staple in your diet. Omega-3 fatty acids, found in fish like salmon and sardines, as well as in flaxseeds and walnuts, are renowned for their anti-inflammatory effects and ability to promote brain health. Antioxidants, too, combat the oxidative stress that is often elevated by chronic stress conditions. Berries, nuts, dark chocolate, and green tea are great sources of antioxidants. Regularly consuming these foods can help fortify your body's defenses against the physical wear and tear caused by stress.

However, maintaining such a diet can be challenging, especially with a busy schedule that might leave little time for meal preparation. This is where effective meal planning becomes essential. Start by setting aside a specific time each week to plan your meals. This doesn't have to be complicated —a simple chart or list outlining what you plan to eat for each meal can suffice. When planning, consider recipes that can be made in bulk and stored, such as stews, casseroles, or salads, ensuring you have nutritious meals readily available throughout the week. Additionally, investing in healthy snacks like fruits, nuts, and yogurt can keep you from reaching for less healthy options when you're short on time.

Avoiding nutritional pitfalls is equally crucial in managing burnout. While high caffeine and sugar intake might provide a temporary energy boost, they often lead to a crash in mood and energy, exacerbating feelings of fatigue. Try to moderate your caffeine consumption and opt for natural sugars from fruits rather than processed snacks. Being mindful of your eating habits—such as not skipping meals and staying hydrated—can also significantly impact your energy levels and ability to cope with stress.

Implementing these nutritional strategies requires mindfulness and commitment, but their benefits in combating burnout are substantial. By nourishing your body with the right foods, planning your meals to fit your schedule, and avoiding detrimental eating habits, you equip yourself with one more essential tool in your arsenal against burnout. This approach enhances your physical well-being and stabilizes your mood and energy levels, enabling you to tackle daily challenges more effectively.

2.6 Physical Activity as a Tool Against Burnout

The restorative power of physical activity in managing and recovering from burnout cannot be overstated. Regular exercise plays a crucial role in diminishing stress hormones like cortisol and adrenaline while simultaneously enhancing the production of endorphins, often referred to as the body's natural painkillers and mood elevators. These biochemical changes improve your overall mood and boost your energy levels, providing a natural counterbalance to the fatigue and lethargy commonly associated with burnout.

Integrating physical activity into your daily routine does not need to be daunting or time-consuming. Simple exercises, when performed consistently, can have profound effects. For instance, incorporating a brisk 15-minute walk into your morning routine can invigorate your start to the day, while periodic stretching sessions throughout the day can help alleviate physical tension and mental stress. Yoga, known for its dual benefits on mind and body, can be particularly effective in managing stress. It combines physical postures, breathing exercises, and meditation to enhance physical flexibility, improve concentration, and promote a calm, clear mind. Tailoring these activities to fit your schedule and fitness level is key. Whether it's a short walk during your lunch break or a yoga session in the evening, the goal is to make physical activity a non-negotiable part of your daily routine.

Building a lasting exercise routine is about understanding and honoring your body's needs and limitations. Start by setting realistic goals based on your current physical condition and time constraints. If you are new to regular exercise, begin with low-impact activities such as walking or gentle yoga and gradually increase the intensity and duration as your fitness improves. Consistency is more beneficial than intensity in the early stages of establishing a routine. Also, consider varying your activities to keep the routine engaging and cover different aspects of fitness, such as cardiovascular health, strength, flexibility, and balance. This variety prevents boredom and ensures a comprehensive approach to physical wellness.

Real-life examples abound of how transformative a regular exercise routine can be in the context of burnout recovery. Take, for instance, Sarah, a graphic designer who found herself overwhelmed by job demands and familial responsibilities. Her introduction to a structured exercise regimen was a turning point. Starting with morning jogs and weekend cycling with friends, Sarah experienced notable improvements in her energy levels and mood. The physical activity relieved her from daily pressures and improved her sleep quality, which enhanced her daily functioning and productivity.

Another example is John, a high school teacher who experienced early signs of burnout, including fatigue and irritability. By integrating swimming into his routine three times a week, he noticed significant reductions in stress and a newfound enthusiasm for his teaching duties. These stories underscore the practical benefits and motivational boost that physical activity can provide, making it an essential component of a holistic approach to managing and recovering from burnout.

Including regular physical exercise in your life offers a dual promise: immediate relief from the day-to-day stresses that contribute to burnout and a long-term strategy for maintaining your mental and physical health. By prioritizing physical activity, you enhance your immediate well-being and build a resilient foundation against future stressors. This approach is not about high-performance athleticism or transforming your body overnight but rather about creating a sustainable practice that supports your overall health and happiness.

As we conclude this chapter on practical recovery strategies, it's clear that the path to overcoming burnout is multifaceted, involving tailored recovery plans, quick stress-relief techniques, nutritional adjustments, professional help, and physical activity. Each strategy plays a unique role in addressing the symptoms of burnout and fortifying your defenses against its recurrence. As you move forward, remember that the ultimate goal is to establish a balanced, fulfilling lifestyle where professional success and personal well-being coexist harmoniously. In the upcoming chapters, we will explore further strategies and insights to support you in this endeavor, ensuring that you have all the tools necessary to lead a vibrant, burnout-free life.

THREE

Tools for Emotional and Psychological Health

I n the intricate dance of daily life, where numerous demands vie for your attention, maintaining emotional and psychological health can sometimes feel like navigating a labyrinth without a map. However, amidst this complexity, there exists a powerful, accessible tool that will guide you through this maze and enhance your journey: mindfulness. Often misconceived as a lofty practice reserved for the serene and secluded, mindfulness is, in fact, a profoundly practical resource that can be woven seamlessly into the fabric of everyday life, offering a wellspring of relief and clarity.

3.1 Mindfulness Practices for Daily Relief

Mindfulness, the art of maintaining a moment-by-moment awareness of our thoughts, feelings, bodily sensations, and surrounding environment, has shown profound efficacy in reducing stress and enhancing emotional regulation. The beauty of mindfulness lies in its simplicity and adaptability;

it can be integrated into daily routines without the need for special equipment or excessive time, making it an ideal practice for those balancing busy schedules.

Integrating mindfulness into your daily life can start with practices as simple as mindful breathing. This technique involves focusing your attention on the breath as it enters and leaves your body, a practice that can be done anywhere at any time, whether you're sitting at your desk, waiting in line, or even during commutes. By anchoring your attention to the rhythm of your breathing, you can cultivate a sense of presence and calm, effectively lowering stress levels and disengaging from habitual thought patterns that may contribute to burnout.

Another accessible mindfulness practice is mindful eating, which involves paying full attention to the experience of eating and drinking inside and outside the body. Mindful eating helps you savor each bite, recognize personal hunger cues, and appreciate your food's colors, smells, textures, and flavors. This practice enhances your eating experience and can lead to more thoughtful dietary choices, contributing to overall well-being.

Mindful walking is yet another practice that can be easily incorporated into your daily regime. It involves walking with awareness of each step and breath, fully engaging with the present moment. Whether walking to your office or taking a brief stroll during a break, mindful walking is a potent antidote to the autopilot mode that often dominates our day-to-day activities, refreshing our mind and invigorating the body.

Benefits of Regular Practice

The benefits of regular mindfulness practice extend far beyond momentary stress relief. Over time, mindfulness helps decrease stress reactivity and enhances emotional regulation, fostering a state of resilience that can buffer you against the challenges of daily life. By regularly engaging in mindfulness exercises, you gradually develop the ability to respond to stressors more thoughtfully rather than react impulsively. This shift not only diminishes the intensity of stress experienced but also enhances your capacity to handle challenging situations with grace and composure.

Furthermore, mindfulness cultivates a deeper, more compassionate connection with oneself. Regular practitioners often report increased self-awareness, which allows for better recognition of personal needs and boundaries, reducing the likelihood of overextension and burnout. This heightened awareness also contributes to improved decision-making and problem-solving abilities, skills that are invaluable in both personal and professional contexts.

Tools and Apps to Assist Practice

In our digital age, numerous tools and applications are available to facilitate mindfulness practice, catering to various preferences and lifestyles. Apps like "Headspace" and "Calm" offer guided mindfulness exercises, including meditations, breathing practices, and sleep stories, which are designed to make mindfulness practice accessible and engaging. These apps provide flexibility in the duration and focus of practices, making incorporating mindfulness into your daily routine easy regardless of your schedule's complexity.

For those who appreciate a more structured approach, digital platforms like "Insight Timer" provide a vast library of guided sessions from mindfulness educators worldwide, offering a range of practices from beginner to advanced levels. These resources support your practice and connect you to a global community of mindfulness practitioners, enhancing your motivation and commitment to regular practice.

Incorporating mindfulness into daily life through simple exercises and the use of supportive digital tools offers a practical and effective strategy for managing stress and enhancing emotional resilience.

3.2 Effective Use of Meditation in Stress Management

Meditation, a practice as ancient as it is profound, offers several benefits for those grappling with the modern epidemic of stress. Rooted in various traditions, meditation has evolved into a tool that transcends cultural boundaries, providing solace and clarity to millions. Meditation is about cultivating a state of mindful presence and awareness, which can significantly diminish the overwhelming noise of everyday life. There are several forms of meditation, each with its specific focus and benefits, which can be tailored to individual needs and preferences.

Focused attention meditation, one of the most traditional forms, involves concentrating on a single reference point. This could be your breath, a specific word, a mantra, or even a candle flame. This practice centers around returning your focus to the chosen object of attention whenever the mind wanders. This form of meditation is particularly beneficial for enhancing concentration and mental clarity. **Mindfulness meditation** contrasts this by encouraging a broad awareness of all aspects of your environment, thoughts, and sensations without attachment. It fosters an enhanced awareness of thought patterns, often leading to greater emotional resilience and decreased reactivity to stress. **Loving-kindness meditation**, or metta, focuses on developing feelings of compassion and love towards oneself and others. It systematically cultivates an attitude of kindness and acceptance, which can be particularly beneficial in reducing negative emotions like anger and frustration.

For those new to meditation, starting a practice can seem daunting. However, the process can be simplified into manageable steps to create a conducive environment for meditation. Begin by finding a quiet space where interruptions are unlikely. Use a comfortable seat—be it a chair, cushion, or mat—where you can sit upright with your back straight yet relaxed. Decide on the duration of your practice, which can be as little as five minutes to start. During your meditation, focus on your breath, a mantra, or whatever you have chosen as your point of focus, and gently guide your attention back whenever you notice it wandering. This practice is not about achieving a state of empty mind but rather about returning to focus, strengthening your attention, and calming your mind.

Many common challenges when starting meditation include difficulty concentrating and finding time within a busy schedule. These obstacles, however, can be addressed with practical solutions. If concentration is an issue, consider shorter, more frequent sessions. Even a few minutes of meditation can be beneficial, and gradually, as your concentration improves, you can extend these periods. Integrating meditation into existing routines can be effective for those struggling with time management. Meditating right after waking up or just before bedtime can anchor the practice in your day without feeling like an additional task.

Real-life case examples further illuminate the transformative potential of regular meditation. Consider the case of a corporate executive who began practicing focused attention meditation to manage work-related stress. Over several months, her concentration improved, allowing her to handle complex projects more efficiently and improve her sleep quality. Another example is a schoolteacher who integrated loving-kindness meditation into his routine, which helped him manage feelings of frustration and impatience, leading to more positive interactions with students and colleagues. These cases underscore the practical benefits of meditation, showing how it can be a vital tool in managing stress and enhancing overall well-being in various professional and personal contexts.

3.3 Cognitive Behavioral Techniques for Self-Help

Cognitive-behavioral therapy (CBT) is a form of psychological treatment that has proven highly effective in combating various mental health disorders, including anxiety, depression, and, crucially for our purposes, burnout. The fundamental premise of CBT lies in the interconnectedness of thoughts, emotions, and behaviors. This therapy posits that our thoughts about a situation influence our emotional response, which in turn can affect our behavior. Changing maladaptive thoughts can alter our emotions and behaviors toward a more positive outcome. Applying the principles of CBT to self-help in managing stress and burnout involves a deep dive into our cognitive processes, identifying negative patterns, and systematically reshaping them towards a healthier mindset.

One of the first steps in this process is self-assessment, where you actively monitor your thoughts and identify those that contribute to stress and feelings of burnout. These thoughts might exaggerate the negatives, underestimate your coping ability, or predict bleak outcomes. Cognitive restructuring, a core component of CBT, involves challenging these negative thoughts and replacing them with more balanced and constructive alternatives. For example, if you frequently find yourself thinking, "I can never meet my deadlines," you might reframe this as, "Sometimes I feel overwhelmed by deadlines, but I have met many in the past, and I can employ strategies to manage my time better." This technique helps alleviate immediate stress and gradually reforms your thought patterns to be more resilient against future stressors.

Behavioral activation is another crucial technique, particularly effective for those experiencing burnout. This strategy encourages you to engage in activities that you find enjoyable or fulfilling, which can be particularly challenging when feeling burnt out. The inertia that comes with burnout often leads to withdrawal from activities that once brought pleasure, only deepening the sense of dissatisfaction and malaise. By actively scheduling these activities into your routine, you counteract the withdrawal by reintroducing positive experiences and emotions into your life. This could be as simple as setting aside time for a hobby you've neglected or committing to a daily walk in nature. The key is to start small and gradually build up as your energy and motivation increase.

For those looking to deepen their understanding and application of CBT, numerous resources are available. Books such as "Feeling Good: The New Mood Therapy" by David D. Burns provide a comprehensive look at the principles of CBT and their application in treating depression. Online courses offered by platforms like Coursera or Udemy can offer more structured learning opportunities, often designed by psychological professionals. These resources not only expand your knowledge but also provide practical tools and strategies that can be tailored to your personal experiences with stress and burnout. Engaging with these materials can empower you with a more active role in managing your mental health, equipped with techniques proven to foster psychological resilience and well-being.

By integrating CBT principles into your self-care regimen, you are taking a proactive step towards recovering from burnout and building a robust mental framework that can withstand the pressures of daily life. This approach offers a promising path to reclaiming your emotional equilibrium and rediscovering the joy in your professional and personal life. As you continue to apply these techniques, observe the transformation in your responses to stress and challenges, marking a significant shift towards a more balanced, fulfilled existence.

3.4 Emotional Intelligence: Understanding and Managing Your Emotions

Emotional Intelligence (EI) is a powerful framework for understanding and managing emotions, both yours and those of others around you. At its core, EI involves a set of skills that can be developed to enhance personal and professional relationships, making interactions more fruitful and less prone to conflict. The concept includes several key components: self-awareness, self-regulation, motivation, empathy, and social skills. Each of these plays a crucial role in how effectively you understand and navigate the social complexities of your life, contributing significantly to personal and professional success and satisfaction.

Self-awareness is the ability to recognize and understand your moods, emotions, and drives and their effect on others. This skill allows you to assess your strengths and limitations accurately, a cornerstone of confidence and self-assurance. Enhancing self-awareness involves journaling your emotional states, reflecting on behaviors that led to successful outcomes or emotional missteps, and seeking feedback from trusted peers or mentors who can provide insights into your interactions and emotional responses.

Self-regulation, which complements self-awareness, involves managing your emotions so that they do not control your behavior or overly influence your decisions. Techniques to improve self-regulation include practicing relaxation methods such as deep breathing or mindfulness meditation, which can help calm emotional turbulence. It also involves setting up an internal system of checks and balances by pausing to consider the potential consequences of your emotional responses before acting on them.

In the context of EI, motivation refers to harnessing your emotions to pursue goals with energy and persistence. High levels of motivation also denote a passion for work that goes beyond money or status and a propensity to pursue goals with energy and persistence. This can be fostered by setting personal and professional goals that are aligned with your values and by ensuring that your roles and responsibilities are challenging yet achievable, providing a steady source of personal satisfaction and accomplishment.

Empathy, or the ability to understand the emotional makeup of other people, is crucial for managing relationships, whether they are personal or professional. It involves more than simply recognizing the emotions of others; it includes developing the ability to put oneself in another's shoes, which can profoundly impact how you interact and respond in various situations. Techniques to enhance empathy include active listening, where the focus is placed entirely on understanding the other person's perspective without immediately preparing a response or judgment.

Social skills in EI are about managing relationships to move people in desired directions, whether that's leading a team, negotiating deals, handling conflicts, or building networks. Developing strong social skills can be achieved by practicing clear communication, learning conflict resolution strategies, and understanding the dynamics of group behavior. This also involves honing persuasive skills, which can help you to motivate others and foster cooperative relationships, thereby enhancing team dynamics and project outcomes.

EI Exercises and Activities

Several practical exercises and activities can be incorporated into your daily routine to actively enhance your emotional intelligence skills. One effective exercise is 'daily reflection,' where, at the end of each day, you reflect on one emotional experience you had and analyze your response to it. Consider what was effective and what could be improved. This practice not only enhances self-awareness but also contributes to better self-regulation.

Another valuable activity is role-playing, which can be particularly effective in developing empathy and social skills. Role-playing various interpersonal scenarios with a friend or colleague allows you to explore different emotional responses and outcomes, providing more in-depth insights into human emotions and how they affect interactions. This exercise can be particularly beneficial in preparing for important conversations or negotiations, as it allows you to anticipate and plan potential emotional reactions from others.

Engaging in group activities or team sports can also be a great way to enhance your social skills. These activities require you to work cooperatively with others, providing a real-world context in which to practice communication, conflict resolution, and collective problem-solving.

By integrating these techniques and activities into your life, you can gradually enhance your emotional intelligence, leading to better stress management, improved relationships at work, and a more fulfilling personal life. This helps prevent burnout and contributes to a more balanced, effective approach to personal challenges and professional engagements. As you continue to develop your EI skills, you may find that your relationships improve, and your overall sense of well-being and effectiveness in various aspects of your life also improves significantly.

3.5 Building Resilience: Preparing for Stress Before It Hits

Resilience, often visualized as the buoyancy that allows some to navigate life's turbulent waters with grace and stamina, is not merely an innate trait but a skill that can be cultivated and strengthened over time. Understanding resilience in the context of psychological and emotional health is crucial; it involves recovering quickly from difficulties, adapting to adversity, and using challenges as opportunities to grow. This capability is especially vital in managing stress and preventing the onset of burnout, acting as a buffer that mitigates the impact of stressors on your mental and physical health.

Building resilience is an active process that involves several key strategies. At the foundation of these strategies is the development of a strong support network. Relationships play a pivotal role in how we manage stress and recover from life's setbacks. A robust support network provides emotional sustenance, practical assistance, and a sense of belonging and community. Cultivating strong, supportive relationships with family, friends, and colleagues can offer a critical lifeline during times of stress. Additionally, engaging in community groups or networks related to your interests can extend your support system and provide new perspectives and resources during challenging times.

Adaptive thinking is another cornerstone of resilience. This strategy involves viewing stressful situations more as challenges to be overcome rather than impassable obstacles. By reframing adversity as an opportunity for growth, you can maintain a hopeful outlook and prevent the kind of negative thought spirals that often precede burnout. Techniques such as cognitive reframing, which encourages identifying and disputing irrational or maladaptive thoughts, can be instrumental in developing this adaptive mindset. Regular practice of adaptive thinking enhances your ability to cope with immediate stressors and contributes to a more persistently positive and resilient outlook on life.

Ensuring physical wellness is equally critical in building resilience. Regular physical activity, adequate sleep, and a nutritious diet all play significant roles in maintaining and enhancing your physical and mental health. Exercise, for instance, strengthens your body and releases endorphins, chemicals in your brain that act as natural painkillers and mood lifters. Adequate sleep replenishes your energy reserves and supports cognitive function and emotional regulation, while a balanced diet provides the necessary nutrients to fuel all your body's processes, helping you to better withstand and recover from stress.

Formal resilience training programs and workshops provide structured guidance and support in developing these skills. These programs often include components such as stress management techniques, problem-solving strategies, and relaxation exercises, all designed to enhance participants' abilities to cope with adversity. Many organizations offer these training sessions as part of their professional development curriculum, recognizing that resilient employees are more adaptable, productive, and less prone to burnout. Universities, community centers, and online platforms also frequently offer resilience workshops that are accessible to the general public, providing valuable resources for anyone looking to bolster their resilience.

The long-term benefits of building resilience are profound. Beyond helping you manage stress, a well-developed resilience skill set prepares you for future challenges, reducing the likelihood of experiencing overwhelming stress or burnout. Resilient individuals are often characterized by a greater capacity for enduring life's ups and downs, maintaining a more stable and positive outlook throughout various life events. This enhances personal well-being and improves professional performance and interpersonal relationships. Over time, the skills associated with resilience, such as adaptive thinking and effective stress management, become ingrained habits that fundamentally shape how you perceive and interact with the world around you.

Cultivating resilience equips you with a toolkit that enhances your current quality of life and prepares you for the future. By building strong relationships, refining your thought processes, maintaining your physical health, and seeking structured training, you lay the foundations for a life characterized by emotional strength and flexibility. This proactive approach to mental and emotional health is a powerful strategy against the pervasive threats of stress and burnout, ensuring that you remain capable of facing life's challenges with confidence and poise.

3.6 Dealing with Anxiety and Depression in Burnout

In the shadows of burnout, anxiety and depression often lurk, subtly intensifying as stress accumulates, often unnoticed until their effects become palpable. Recognizing the symptoms of these conditions early in the context of burnout is crucial for the individual's well-being and the effectiveness of any recovery plan. Anxiety in the realm of burnout might manifest as persistent worry about work performance, a pervasive sense of apprehension about the future, or physical symptoms such as an increased heart rate, excessive sweating, or gastrointestinal issues. Depression related to burnout often appears as a deep fatigue that rest doesn't alleviate, a profound sadness or indifference towards work achievements, and a general withdrawal from social interactions.

The importance of addressing these symptoms promptly cannot be overstated. Left unchecked, anxiety and depression can prolong the duration of burnout and severely impact your quality of life, leading to deteriorated health, strained relationships, and decreased productivity. Early intervention strategies are key and should include techniques tailored to manage these specific symptoms. For anxiety, strategies might include structured relaxation techniques such as progressive muscle relaxation or guided imagery, which help calm the mind and reduce the physical symptoms of anxiety. Cognitive-behavioral techniques, such as challenging irrational fears and learning to control worry, are also effective.

For depression, interventions might include activities that boost mood and engagement, such as regular physical exercise and scheduling pleasant activities that you can look forward to each day. Additionally, maintaining a consistent daily routine can help combat the feelings of aimlessness and helplessness that often accompany depression. It's essential to monitor the effectiveness of these strategies closely and consider professional help if symptoms persist or worsen. Seeking help from a mental health professional, such as a psychologist or psychiatrist, can provide you with additional strategies and support tailored to your specific needs, and in some cases, medication may be recommended as part of your treatment plan.

Integrating mental health care into your burnout recovery plan is a critical step that should be approached holistically. It's not merely about treating symptoms but about understanding and addressing the root causes of your stress and emotional distress. This holistic approach includes looking at all aspects of your life, from your work environment and personal relationships to your physical health and coping strategies. Mental health professionals can work with you to create a comprehensive plan that addresses these various areas, helping to ensure a balanced and sustainable recovery.

Support systems are indispensable in recovery, providing emotional and practical assistance. Knowing that you have people who care about you and can offer a listening ear, or a helping hand can make a significant difference in your recovery journey. Resources such as support groups, either in person or online, can also be incredibly beneficial. These groups provide a sense of community and understanding that can be incredibly comforting. You realize you are not alone in your struggles, and you can share strategies and encouragement with others who understand what you are going through.

Professional resources are equally important. If you're struggling with symptoms of anxiety or depression as part of burnout, mental health professionals such as therapists or counselors are invaluable. They can offer a range of therapies and treatments tailored to your specific needs. Additionally, many workplaces now offer employee assistance programs (EAPs) that provide access to mental health services. These services can be a great starting point for anyone feeling overwhelmed by anxiety or depression related to burnout.

In summary, recognizing the signs of anxiety and depression within the context of burnout and taking early action to address them is crucial. By integrating effective intervention strategies, holistic mental health care, and robust support systems into your recovery plan, you are laying a strong foundation for overcoming burnout and restoring your health and well-being. As we move forward, remember that recovery is not just about getting back to where you were before burnout; it's about building a new way of living that supports your ongoing health and happiness. This approach ensures that you are not just surviving but thriving, both now and in the future.

FOUR

Achieving Work-Life Balance

In the modern professional landscape, the quest for a harmonious work-life balance often seems like a mythic pursuit. The ever-blurring lines between work responsibilities and personal life can leave you feeling as though you're perpetually treading water, struggling to keep your head above the myriad demands. Yet, the importance of establishing and maintaining a balance is not just about preventing burnout; it's about cultivating a life that allows space for both achievement and joy, productivity and relaxation. As we delve into this chapter, we will explore practical, actionable strategies designed to help you navigate this delicate balance, ensuring that you thrive professionally and personally.

4.1 Setting Boundaries: Practical Steps

Defining Boundaries and Their Significance

Boundaries are the psychological and physical limits we set to protect our well-being. They help differentiate our needs, desires, and preferences from others, serving as a crucial mechanism for maintaining our mental health and job satisfaction. In the workplace, boundaries prevent professional responsibilities from encroaching on personal time and space, which is essential for reducing stress and preventing burnout. Clear boundaries enable you to delegate your energy and time effectively, enhancing productivity while preserving time for rest and personal pursuits.

Steps to Establish Clear Boundaries

The process of setting boundaries at work begins with self-reflection. Identify the aspects of your job that encroach upon your personal life. Is it the expectation to respond to emails late at night? Or perhaps the tendency to bring work home over the weekends? Once identified, articulate these boundaries clearly and assertively to your colleagues and superiors. For instance, you might decide that you will not check emails after 7 PM or on weekends. Communicate this decision clearly to your team and supervisors, perhaps through a conversation or an email setting out your availability and expected response times.

When communicating these boundaries, be direct yet respectful, explaining how this will help you maintain productivity and engagement during designated work hours.

It's also helpful to provide alternatives for urgent communications, such as a phone call during your off-hours, which respects your boundaries while acknowledging your team's or clients' needs.

Handling Boundary Pushback

Setting boundaries might initially be met with resistance, especially if late hours and constant availability have been the norm. When faced with pushback, maintain your stance but be open to dialogue. Use assertive communication techniques to express your needs without aggression or passivity. For example, if a superior insists on late-night emails, you might respond with, "I understand the urgency of our projects, but I perform best when I can disconnect in the evenings. Can we find a way to prioritize emails during work hours or discuss urgent matters via phone if something can't wait until the next day?"

Evaluating and Adjusting Boundaries

Boundaries aren't set in stone; they should evolve as your work and personal life change. Regularly review the effectiveness of your boundaries—Are they helping you manage stress? Do they allow for sufficient downtime? Adjust them as needed and keep the line of communication open with your colleagues about why these boundaries are necessary. It's important that they see these adjustments not as a rigid barrier but as a way for you to work more effectively.

Interactive Element: Boundary Setting Worksheet

To aid in setting and maintaining effective work boundaries, below is a worksheet to help you articulate and plan your boundaries:

1. Identify Boundary Needs: List the areas where you need to set boundaries (e.g., time, physical space, communication).
2. Define Specific Boundaries: For each area listed, specify your boundary (e.g., no work emails after 7 p.m.).
3. Plan Communication: Outline how you will communicate these boundaries to your colleagues and what language you will use.
4. Feedback and Adjustment Strategy: Decide how you will gather feedback on these boundaries and the frequency of reviewing and adjusting them.

This tool is designed to help you establish boundaries that safeguard your personal time while maintaining professional effectiveness. By clearly articulating and consistently applying these boundaries, you create a work environment that respects your professional commitments and personal well-being, setting the stage for a balanced, fulfilling life.

4.2 Time Management Skills for the Overwhelmed

In the whirlwind of daily responsibilities, effective time management is your anchor, helping you navigate tasks precisely and calmly. Particularly for those feeling overwhelmed, mastering the art of organizing your day can transform chaos into a structured flow of productivity and peace. This transformation begins with prioritization, a critical skill that lets you distinguish between what must be done immediately and what can wait, aligning your efforts with the most impactful activities first.

The Eisenhower Box, a simple yet powerful tool for prioritizing tasks, divides your activities into four categories based on their urgency and importance. Both urgent and important tasks should be done immediately, as these typically relate to critical deadlines or emergencies. Important but not urgent tasks should be scheduled for later, allowing you to plan strategically without the pressure of an impending deadline. On the other hand, urgent but unimportant tasks can be delegated to others, ensuring that your focus remains on high-impact activities. Lastly, tasks that are neither urgent nor important should be set aside or eliminated, as they are likely distractions that do not contribute meaningfully to your goals.

Incorporating tools and apps specifically designed for time management can further enhance your ability to navigate your workload effectively. Apps like 'Todoist' or 'Trello' allow you to organize tasks into projects, set deadlines, and monitor progress, all within a user-friendly interface. These tools keep you aligned with your daily to-dos and provide visual satisfaction as you check off completed tasks, reinforcing your sense of accomplishment. Additionally, apps like 'Focus@Will' offer productivity-enhancing music tailored to your work habits, while 'Forest' gamifies the process of staying focused, rewarding you with a growing virtual tree for each period you resist the temptation to check your phone.

Building a structured daily schedule is another cornerstone of effective time management. This structure should encompass your professional tasks and allocate time for personal activities and breaks, ensuring a well-rounded day. Start by defining the hours you intend to dedicate to work, ideally, those when you feel most productive. Designate time blocks for specific tasks within this work period, using your prioritized list as a guide. Equally important is scheduling breaks; regular intervals for rest and rejuvenation are crucial for maintaining high levels of efficiency throughout the day. These breaks can include a short walk, a meditation session, or simply a moment to step away from your workspace and clear your mind.

To truly tailor your schedule to your personal and professional needs, consider performing a time audit. This process involves tracking how you spend your time over a week, noting each activity and its duration. By the end of the week, analyze this data to identify patterns or time sinks — activities that consume a disproportionate amount of time relative to their importance. This insight allows you to make informed adjustments to your habits, perhaps reducing the time allocated to checking emails or eliminating unnecessary meetings. The goal of this audit is not to create a rigid schedule but to develop a flexible plan that best supports your productivity and well-being.

By adopting these time management strategies — prioritizing tasks using the Eisenhower Box, leveraging digital tools, structuring your day, and conducting time audits — you equip yourself with the skills necessary to manage your responsibilities efficiently without succumbing to the pressure and chaos that often lead to overwhelm. As you implement these techniques, observe the changes in your work output and overall sense of control and satisfaction, marking a significant step towards a balanced and productive life.

4.3 The Art of Saying No: Empowerment without Guilt

One of the most nuanced yet powerful skills you can cultivate in both your professional and personal life is the ability to say no. This simple act, often laden with undue guilt and anxiety, is fundamentally about honoring your own needs and capacity. The reluctance to decline requests typically stems from deep-seated fears—fear of conflict, disappointing others, or jeopardizing relationships. Yet, learning to say no is not just about rejecting something; it is also about saying yes to your own well-being and priorities. Embracing this skill can lead to a profound sense of empowerment, as it allows you to make choices that align with your personal and professional goals, ultimately fostering a healthier, more balanced life.

Understanding the psychological barriers that prevent saying no is the first step towards overcoming them. Many people fear that saying no will lead to conflict or will damage relationships. This fear is often rooted in a natural human desire to be liked and accepted by peers and superiors. However, always saying yes can lead to overcommitment, stress, and resentment, which are far more detrimental to personal health and professional relationships than a well-placed no. Additionally, there is the misconception that saying no is a sign of non-cooperation or laziness, whereas, in reality, it can be a sign of a person who knows their limits and is committed to delivering high-quality work within those boundaries.

To navigate these challenges, specific phrases and techniques can be employed to say no effectively while maintaining professionalism and respect. Begin by acknowledging the request; show that you understand its importance. For instance, you might say, "I understand this project is a priority, and it sounds like an exciting challenge." Follow this with a concise and honest explanation of why you cannot accommodate the request. For example, "However, given my current commitments, I wouldn't be able to devote the necessary time to deliver the standard of work required." Offering an alternative or a compromise, such as suggesting a later time or delegating the task to someone else, can also be helpful. You might add, "I can revisit this next month, or perhaps Sam might have the capacity to take this on now."

Balancing the needs of your team or organization with your personal limits is crucial. This balance requires a clear assessment of when saying no is necessary to protect your time and mental health. Begin by evaluating your current workload and priorities. Consider whether the new request aligns with your primary responsibilities and goals. If it doesn't, and if taking it on would overload you or distract you from your main duties, these are valid grounds for a refusal. It's also important to consider the cumulative impact of your work; sometimes, taking on just one more task can tip the balance from manageable to overwhelming.

Dealing with the guilt or anxiety that might follow when saying no is another aspect that needs attention. Feelings of guilt often stem from a misplaced sense of obligation or a personal standard that equates busyness with productivity and worth. To counteract these feelings, remind yourself of the reasons for your decision. Reflect on the potential consequences if you had said yes—increased stress, potential burnout, and perhaps even a decline in the quality of your work. Remember, saying no can often be the more responsible choice, preserving your ability to perform well in your existing commitments. Additionally, practicing self-compassion is key. Recognize that you are human, with limited time and energy, and it is not only okay but necessary to set limits for yourself.

By embracing the art of saying no, you empower yourself to manage your professional and personal life more effectively. This skill, while simple, supports a sustainable career and enriches your overall well-being, allowing you to contribute your best where it matters most. As you continue to practice and refine this skill, you'll find that the initial discomfort associated with saying no diminishes, replaced by a confident assurance in your ability to make decisions that honor your capacities and commitments.

4.4 Remote Work and Burnout: Managing New Challenges

The shift to remote work has transformed the landscape of professional life, introducing a new set of challenges that, if not managed carefully, can lead to burnout. The very benefits of remote work—flexibility and the absence of a commute—can also become detrimental without proper boundaries. Isolation, the blurring of lines between personal and professional life, and the tendency to overwork are predominant challenges that many face when working from home. Addressing these effectively enhances productivity and safeguards your mental health.

Isolation is one of the most significant challenges associated with remote work. Removed from the bustling environment of an office, you may miss the informal conversations that break up the monotony of the workday and serve as a casual barometer for measuring stress levels and workload among peers. Over time, this lack of interaction can contribute to feelings of loneliness and detachment, which are potent precursors to burnout. To counteract this, creating opportunities for engagement with colleagues is vital. Regular virtual meetings can help, but it's also beneficial to facilitate less formal interactions, such as virtual coffee breaks or remote social events, which can recreate the camaraderie that naturally develops in an office environment.

Another significant challenge is the blurring of boundaries between work and personal life, which can lead to overworking. Without the physical separation of an office environment, you might find yourself checking emails late at night or during meals, gradually extending your work hours. To combat this, establishing a dedicated workspace is crucial. This space should be reserved solely for work, whether it's a separate room or just a specific corner of your living area. This physical separation helps condition your brain to enter 'work mode' when you're in this space and, importantly, to switch off when you leave it. Equally crucial is setting strict start and end times for your workday. Communicate these boundaries clearly to your colleagues to ensure they respect your off-hours, reinforcing these boundaries with consistent behavior—such as not responding to non-urgent communications outside work hours.

In addition to physical setup and structured schedules, the effective use of technology plays a pivotal role in managing remote work challenges. Technology should be a tool that supports work-life balance rather than a tool that hinders it. Utilize digital tools that streamline communication and collaboration, such as project management software and online communication platforms, which can reduce the need for constant check-ins and updates, thereby decreasing stress and distraction. Tools that integrate calendars and allow you to visually plot out your day can be particularly helpful in managing your time effectively. For instance, blocking out time for deep work, as well as breaks and personal time, can help you maintain a healthier balance and reduce the risk of burnout.

Furthermore, technology can also be leveraged to maintain and even enhance the social interactions that are often missing in remote work settings. Encourage the use of video calls for meetings to facilitate face-to-face interaction and consider setting up virtual 'water coolers'—dedicated times and virtual spaces for team members to gather informally. These interactions are vital for building and maintaining a sense of community and support that can mitigate feelings of isolation and disconnection.

Managing remote work effectively requires a deliberate structuring of your work environment and schedule to ensure that the flexibility of working from home does not turn into a free-for-all that ultimately leads to burnout. By setting clear boundaries, utilizing technology wisely, and maintaining regular social interactions, you can create a remote working experience that supports both productivity and well-being. This proactive approach allows you to enjoy the benefits of remote work while managing its unique challenges, ensuring that your professional life remains both fulfilling and sustainable.

4.5 Negotiating Workload and Responsibilities

Navigating the complexities of modern work environments often requires you to manage a diverse array of tasks and responsibilities. At times, the volume or difficulty of these tasks can exceed your capacity, leading to stress and potential burnout. Assessing your workload effectively is the first step toward achieving a sustainable balance. Begin by cataloging your current tasks, distinguishing between those that are essential and those that may be less critical. Consider factors such as deadlines, the consequences of not completing tasks, and the amount of effort required for each. This assessment helps clarify your immediate priorities and illuminates areas where the expectations placed upon you may not align with your capabilities or resources.

Once you clearly understand your workload, the next crucial step involves communication strategies for discussing workload adjustments with your supervisors. Approach this conversation with a focus on solutions rather than problems. For instance, rather than simply stating that your workload is too heavy, prepare to propose feasible adjustments. This might involve suggesting a reprioritization of tasks, extending deadlines, or redistributing certain responsibilities. When presenting your case, be specific about how these adjustments will enable you to perform more effectively, benefiting you, the team, and the organization. It's important to convey these points in a manner that underscores your commitment to your role and your interest in maximizing your contributions to the team.

Delegation is another key strategy in managing an excessive workload. It involves determining which tasks can be transferred to others without compromising the quality of work. Effective delegation requires a good understanding of the strengths and capacities of your colleagues. When choosing tasks to delegate, consider which responsibilities others can perform efficiently, perhaps even more so than yourself. This lightens your load and helps develop your team members' skills and capacities. When delegating, be clear about the expected outcomes and provide the necessary resources and support to complete the tasks. This ensures that delegation is beneficial and does not merely shift the burden of stress from one person to another.

Creating a supportive work culture where discussions about workload and stress are normalized and encouraged can have profound benefits for all employees. Such a culture fosters openness and mutual support, where team members feel comfortable expressing concerns about workload without fear of negative repercussions. This environment can be cultivated by leadership through regular check-ins with team members, providing platforms for feedback, and actively demonstrating a commitment to employee well-being. Workshops and training sessions on time management, stress reduction, and effective communication can also equip employees with the tools they need to manage their workloads more effectively and support their colleagues in doing the same.

In fostering such a culture, it's crucial that all team members, including management, model these practices. Leaders who openly discuss their own strategies for managing workload and stress effectively give permission to others to do the same. This reduces the stigma around discussing workload concerns and builds a team ethos of shared responsibility for maintaining a healthy work environment. As these practices become ingrained in the organizational culture, they contribute to a more resilient workforce capable of handling the demands of the job without succumbing to burnout. This proactive approach to workload management enhances individual well-being and drives the overall productivity and morale of the team, creating a win-win situation for employees and the organization alike.

4.6 Preventing Burnout in High-Pressure Careers

In high-pressure careers where the stakes are monumental and the hours long, the risk of burnout looms larger than in more routine or less intense professions. Individuals in these roles often face a constant barrage of demands that require their time and immediate intellectual and emotional engagement. From surgeons and corporate lawyers to high-ranking executives and entrepreneurs, the relentless pressure to perform at peak capacity without error or delay can rapidly deplete mental and physical reserves.

Key factors that contribute to burnout in such high-stakes environments include prolonged working hours that encroach on time for personal restoration, high emotional and cognitive demands that drain mental resources, and a perpetual state of 'on-call' availability that leaves little room for disengagement from work pressures. Combined, these elements create a perfect storm for burnout, manifesting in diminished work performance and deteriorating personal health and relationships.

To effectively manage stress in these intense settings, professionals can employ tailored strategies that acknowledge and address the unique challenges of their roles. One effective approach is to establish ultra-clear priorities. This involves identifying the most impactful tasks and understanding and articulating your highest personal and professional values, which can guide decision-making and effort allocation. This clarity helps in distinguishing between what is truly crucial and what can be deferred, delegated, or dropped, thus preserving your energy for the most meaningful engagements.

Maintaining robust professional support networks is also vital. These networks can provide emotional backing and practical assistance during particularly challenging periods. They can be formal, such as mentorship programs within your industry, or informal, such as peer groups or professional friendships that offer a safe space for sharing challenges and strategies. These relationships provide solace, understanding, diverse perspectives, and solutions you may not have considered.

Regular mental health check-ins are another cornerstone of preventing burnout in high-pressure jobs. This practice involves periodically assessing your mental health status to catch early signs of stress, anxiety, or depression. Whether through self-assessment tools or consultations with mental health professionals, these check-ins can prompt necessary adjustments in your work habits or coping strategies before full-blown burnout develops. Many high-performing professionals engage in regular sessions with psychologists or coaches who specialize in high-stress careers, which helps them maintain their mental wellness despite the demands of their jobs.

Case Studies from High-Pressure Professionals

The real-life experiences of individuals who have managed to navigate the treacherous waters of high-pressure careers while avoiding burnout provide both inspiration and practical blueprints for others. Consider the case of Dr. Lisa, a cardiac surgeon who, after years of grueling hours and emotionally charged operations, began to feel the onset of burnout. Recognizing the warning signs, she took proactive steps to restructure her schedule, prioritizing her most demanding surgeries earlier in the week and setting aside Fridays for administrative tasks and patient consultations, which required a different kind of focus. She also established a weekly debrief with a mentor, where she could discuss cases and her feelings about them, helping her process the emotional load of her work.

Another example is from the corporate world: Michael, a senior software engineer, implemented a strict routine that segmented his work into highly focused sprints followed by short breaks. He used techniques like the Pomodoro Technique to maintain this discipline, which improved his productivity and ensured he regularly stepped away from his desk to recharge. Furthermore, Michael set boundaries around his availability, communicating clearly to his team that he was not available for calls or emails after 7 PM or on weekends unless in cases of absolute emergency. This helped him recover from work stress during his downtime and encouraged his team to solve problems more autonomously.

These stories underscore the necessity and effectiveness of strategic planning, support networks, and mental health maintenance in managing the demands of high-pressure careers. Setting clear priorities, fostering supportive professional relationships, and monitoring mental health closely can help one thrive even in the most challenging environments without succumbing to burnout.

As this chapter concludes, it's clear that the strategies discussed here are not just about managing workload or stress but fundamentally rethinking how we engage with our high-pressure roles. By proactively setting priorities, building support systems, and routinely checking in on our mental health, we can protect ourselves from burnout, ensuring our successful and sustainable careers. As we transition to the next chapter, we will explore additional strategies that further enhance our ability to maintain balance and wellness in our professional lives, ensuring that we continue to perform at our best without compromising our health and happiness.

Make a Difference with Your Review

"Giving is not just about making a donation. It is about making a difference."

Kathy Calvin

Helping others without expecting anything in return makes us happier and can even prolong our lives. So, if we can make a difference together, let's go for it!

I have a simple question for you...

Would you help someone you've never met, even if you never got credit for it?

This person is a lot like you. Or maybe how you used to be. They are looking for ways to make their life better, reduce stress, and improve their health, but they need some guidance.

My mission is to make conquering burnout easy for everyone. Everything I do stems from that mission. And, to reach as many people as possible, I need your help.

Most people do judge a book by its cover and by its reviews. So, here's my request on behalf of someone who needs help:

Please leave a review for this book.

Your review costs no money and takes less than 60 seconds, but it can change someone's life. Your review could help...

- one more person find ways to reduce their stress.
- one more person improve their health.
- one more person strengthen their relationships.
- one more person feel happier and more energetic.
- one more person conquer burnout.

To feel good about helping someone, all you need to do is leave a review. It takes less than 60 seconds.

Simply scan the QR code to leave your review:

If you enjoy helping others, you are my kind of person. Welcome to the club. You're one of us.

I am excited to help you reduce your stress, nurture your relationships, and improve your overall health and wellness. You'll love the tips and strategies in the coming chapters.

Thank you from the bottom of my heart. Now, back to our regularly scheduled program.

Your biggest fan,

M.L. Winters

PS - Fun fact: When you help others, it makes you feel even better. If you know someone who could use this book, share it with them.

FIVE

Enhancing Relationship and Social Connections

I n the intricate tapestry of life, our relationships profoundly influence our well-being, shaping our experiences and coloring our perceptions of the world. Whether these connections are familial, romantic, or professional, their health directly impacts our own, particularly in managing stress and preventing burnout. This chapter delves into the critical role of effective communication in nurturing these relationships, ensuring they remain sources of support rather than stress. By mastering the art of conveying needs and boundaries, you can cultivate enduring and thriving relationships, even in the face of life's inevitable pressures.

5.1 Communicating Needs and Boundaries in Relationships

The Importance of Clear Communication

At the heart of every healthy relationship lies clear communication. The bridge connects understanding to action, ensuring all parties are aligned and minimizing misunder-standings. When you articulate your needs and boundaries clearly, you invite an open dialogue that fosters trust and mutual respect. This clarity prevents the accumulation of unspoken frustrations—which can lead to resentment and emotional distance—and empowers all involved to interact more empathetically. By explicitly stating what you can tolerate and what you expect from the relationship, you set a clear framework within which it can dynamically grow and adapt.

Effective communication in relationships involves more than just talking about your day or sharing your thoughts. It requires the courage to express needs that might be complex or evolving and the clarity to define boundaries that safe-guard your emotional and mental well-being. For instance, if you are someone who values quiet time after a long workday, communicating this need helps your partner understand that this preference is not a rejection but a necessary aspect of your self-care. Similarly, by setting boundaries around work-related calls at home, you help your family understand how they can support you in maintaining a balance that benefits everyone.

Strategies for Effective Communication

To communicate effectively, start by being as specific and direct as possible about your needs and boundaries. Use "I" statements to express your feelings and avoid blame. For example, say, "I feel overwhelmed when I don't have any downtime after work, and I need an hour to myself," rather than "You don't give me any space." This approach reduces defensiveness and enhances your autonomy over your feelings and needs.

Active listening plays a crucial role in effective communication. This means fully concentrating on what is being said rather than just passively hearing the words. Reflect on what your partner or colleague says and clarify their statements by asking questions. This indicates that you value their input and are engaged in the conversation, paving the way for a more in-depth understanding and stronger connection.

Another useful strategy is to practice assertiveness, which involves expressing your thoughts and feelings confidently and respectfully. Assertiveness allows you to advocate for your needs while considering the needs of others, creating a balanced dialogue where solutions can be mutually negotiated.

Role-Play Scenarios

To help you visualize and practice effective communication strategies, consider these role-play scenarios:

1. Scenario: You must decline additional work projects to manage your stress levels.

- Role-Play: Explain to your supervisor, "I am currently at capacity with my existing projects, and I want to maintain the quality of my output. Can we discuss priorities and perhaps adjust deadlines or redistribute some tasks?"

2. Scenario: You require personal time at family gatherings to step away and decompress.

- Role-Play: Communicate to your family, "I enjoy our time together, but I also need short breaks to recharge. I will take a quick walk outside to clear my mind and then rejoin everyone refreshed."

Handling Resistance

When communicating your needs and boundaries, you might encounter resistance or negative reactions. It's important to stay calm and empathetic when these situations arise. Reaffirm your boundaries with a firm yet gentle tone and express your willingness to find a compromise if possible. For example, if a colleague resists your request not to be disturbed during certain hours, you might suggest alternative times when you are available for discussions or offer to check in periodically.

Remember, setting boundaries aims not to alienate others but to foster healthier, more sustainable interactions. By consistently applying these communication strategies, you demonstrate commitment to your well-being and the health of your relationships, creating a supportive network that enhances your resilience against stress and burnout. As you continue to apply these principles, observe the positive changes in your interactions and the increased harmony in your relationships, reflecting a profound understanding and respect for each other's needs and boundaries.

5.2 The Role of Social Support in Burnout Recovery

Social support serves as a crucial buffer against the stresses that precipitate burnout, offering solace and practical aid during challenging times. Imagine social support as a safety net; it's there to catch you when life's professional and personal demands threaten to sweep you off your feet. The presence of a supportive network can significantly lighten your emotional load by providing empathy, understanding, and concrete assistance, which can be pivotal during periods of intense stress or when navigating the path to recovery from burnout.

A robust social support network typically comprises various relationships, each offering different forms of support. Family members often provide emotional support and practical help, such as taking on household duties when you're overwhelmed. Friends can offer a listening ear and an escape from the pressures of work, reminding you of life outside your responsibilities. Colleagues and professional peers, understanding the unique stresses of your work environment, can offer validation and strategies for managing workplace stress. Professional groups or associations can also be invaluable, offering resources and networking opportunities that can reduce professional isolation and provide guidance and support through shared experiences.

Cultivating and maintaining these support networks, however, requires intentional effort. Start by reaching out and nurturing relationships that provide mutual support. Regular check-ins via calls, texts, or meet-ups can keep these connections strong. Be proactive in your interactions; rather than waiting for support, be the one to offer it. This reciprocity builds stronger bonds and establishes a foundation of trust and mutual respect, which is essential for a supportive relationship. Additionally, participating in community or professional groups can broaden your support network. These groups often hold meetings or social events that provide opportunities to connect with others who share similar interests or challenges.

Integrating professional or therapeutic support into your personal support network can also play a critical role in your recovery from burnout. Therapists or counselors can provide a safe space to explore your feelings and challenges, offering professional insights and coping strategies that are tailored to your specific needs. If you're hesitant to seek professional help, consider starting with support groups in person or online. These groups provide a platform to share your experiences and learn from others facing similar issues, which can be incredibly validating and reassuring.

Effectively utilizing professional support involves being open and honest about your struggles and actively engaging in the therapeutic process. It's important to view professional help not as a last resort but as a proactive step toward maintaining your mental health. Regular sessions with a mental therapist can provide continuity of care and allow you to navigate the ups and downs of recovery with professional guidance. As mentioned in Chapter 3, many employers offer Employee Assistance Programs (EAPs) that provide access to counseling services, which can be a convenient and confidential way to receive support.

Building and maintaining a diverse and robust support network is a dynamic process that adapts to your changing needs and circumstances. Investing in these relationships and utilizing available resources strengthens your resilience against stress and burnout, ensuring that you have a solid network of support to rely on when challenges arise. As you continue to nurture these connections, remember that the strength of your support network lies not just in the number of connections you have but in the quality and depth of those relationships.

5.3 Rebuilding Connections: Steps to Revitalize Your Social Life

Rekindling the vibrancy of your social life after experiencing burnout requires a conscious effort to reengage with the world around you. Burnout often leaves you feeling disconnected, not just from your work but also from your social circles. You might find that your interactions have dwindled, not out of desire, but due to the exhaustive demands that led to your burnout. The process of revitalizing your social engagements is akin to tending a garden that's been left untended—requiring patience, care, and thoughtful planning.

Start by assessing your current level of social interaction. Reflect on your interactions over the past few weeks and note their frequency and quality. Ask yourself: Are these interactions fulfilling? Do they energize me or leave me feeling drained? This reflection helps identify what's missing or what might be too overwhelming in your social life. It's not uncommon to discover that while certain interactions have lapsed, others might need to be adjusted to better suit your current state of recovery. This assessment forms the groundwork on which you can begin to build a more fulfilling social structure.

Planning for re-engagement with your social circles should be approached with intention but also with flexibility. Begin by identifying activities or groups that align with your interests and are likely to support your recovery rather than drain your energy. This might mean prioritizing small gatherings involving close friends rather than large social events. Consider activities that you've previously enjoyed or have always wanted to try. The key here is to choose engagements that feel enriching and manageable, not those that feel like obligations. Slowly integrate these into your schedule, starting perhaps with a bi-weekly coffee meet-up with a friend, gradually increasing as you feel more comfortable and energized.

For many recovering from burnout, the prospect of socializing can evoke anxiety or hesitation—a natural response when you've been out of the social loop due to mental and emotional exhaustion. Overcoming this anxiety is crucial and can be managed through gradual exposure combined with positive reinforcement. Before attending a social event, take time to prepare mentally. Remind yourself of the benefits of reconnecting and the joy that meaningful interactions can bring. During social interactions, stay mindful of your energy levels and allow yourself to step back if you feel overwhelmed. After each positive social experience, take a moment to reflect on what went well and how it made you feel, reinforcing the positive aspects of reconnecting.

Balancing social life with the need for personal downtime is critical. It's important to listen to your body and mind and recognize when you need to recharge alone. This balance is not static; it will shift as you recover from burnout and as your social stamina improves. Establishing and maintaining boundaries around your personal time will help ensure that your social life enriches rather than exhausts you. Communicate openly with friends and family about your need for balance and plan your social calendar in a way that includes ample downtime. This might mean having a 'quiet day' after a social event or scheduling certain days of the week as 'no plans' days to ensure you have time to rest and recuperate.

Navigating the path to a revitalized social life post-burnout is a journey of rediscovery—of your interests, social needs, and interactions that fulfill you. It requires an understanding that while social connections are a source of joy and support, they must be managed thoughtfully to ensure they contribute positively to your life. With patience and careful planning, you can rebuild a social life that supports your recovery and enhances your overall well-being.

5.4 Managing Relationship Stress to Prevent Burnout

Navigating through the complexities of relationships, whether they are personal, professional, or social, often involves dealing with stressors that can significantly impact your mental health and contribute to burnout if not managed effectively. Common sources of stress within relationships include unmet expectations, financial disagreements, lack of communication, and misaligned life goals. By fostering resentment and misunderstanding, these stressors can create a breeding ground for conflict and emotional tension. Recognizing and addressing these sources of stress early can help in maintaining the health of your relationships and preventing the onset of burnout.

Conflict is a natural part of any relationship; however, its impact depends largely on how it is handled. Effective conflict resolution plays a crucial role in maintaining harmony and reducing stress. One effective strategy is focusing on the issue rather than the person. This approach helps in addressing the problem without making the other person feel attacked, which can escalate the conflict. For instance, if a disagreement arises over financial spending, discuss the specific spending behaviors that concern you rather than criticizing the person's character or intentions. It's also beneficial to seek a compromise where possible. This shows a willingness to work together towards a solution that respects both parties' needs, fostering cooperation and understanding.

Another technique involves using a 'time-out' when emotions run high. Maintaining clarity and perspective can be challenging During a heated argument. You can prevent the situation from worsening by agreeing to pause and revisit the discussion once both parties have calmed down. During this time-out, engage in activities that help you calm down and gather your thoughts, such as deep breathing, a short walk, or meditation. This break can provide the necessary space to approach the issue more constructively.

Empathy and understanding are vital in navigating the emotional landscape of relationships. By striving to see the situation from the other person's perspective, you can gain insights into their feelings and motivations, which can alter your perception of the conflict. This doesn't mean you have to agree with their viewpoint, but understanding it can help find common ground and resolve disagreements more amicably. Practicing empathy also involves acknowledging the other person's feelings and expressing your understanding. For example, you might say, "I see that this really frustrates you," or "It sounds like you feel overlooked." These expressions of empathy can validate their feelings and open up space for more open and productive communication.

Maintaining your own mental health and well-being is equally crucial in managing relationship stress. This involves recognizing your emotional limits and ensuring you do not compromise your health to sustain a relationship. Engage regularly in self-care practices that recharge your emotional and physical energy. This might include activities like reading, exercising, or pursuing a hobby. Keeping yourself mentally and physically fit allows you to interact more positively and effectively with others, reducing the likelihood of conflicts escalating into significant stressors.

Additionally, it's important to cultivate a support network outside your immediate relationships. This network, which might include friends, family, or a support group, can provide objective perspectives and emotional support when dealing with relationship stress. Sometimes, talking through your feelings and frustrations with someone removed from the situation can provide clarity and new solutions.

In managing relationship stress, the goal is to create a balance where your relationships are sources of support and joy rather than chronic stress. By employing effective conflict resolution strategies, practicing empathy, and prioritizing self-care, you can foster healthier interactions that contribute to your overall well-being and protect against burnout. As you continue to develop these skills, you will likely find that your relationships improve and your resilience against stress strengthens, enabling you to face life's challenges with greater confidence and equanimity.

5.5 Networking and Social Skills as Tools Against Isolation

In the vast expanse of professional life, networking emerges as a ladder to career advancement and a vital antidote to the isolation that often accompanies modern work environments. The value of expanding your professional network extends beyond the mere exchange of business cards or LinkedIn connections. It fosters a sense of belonging and mutual support, crucial for those navigating the solitary waters of freelance work, remote roles, or high-pressure careers. You gain access to a community that shares your professional interests and challenges through networking, offering a wellspring of collaboration and support. These interactions often lead to mentorship, partnership, and even friendship opportunities, which can significantly diminish feelings of professional isolation and enhance your career satisfaction.

Building and nurturing a professional network requires a set of social skills that can be systematically developed and refined. Among these, active listening stands out as one of the most critical. This skill involves fully concentrating on the speaker, understanding their message, responding appropriately, and remembering the information later. In networking scenarios, active listening can help you identify potential areas of collaboration or support, making your interactions more productive and meaningful. It also signals respect and interest, laying the groundwork for strong professional relationships.

Small talk, often overlooked as superficial, is another essential tool in your networking arsenal. It serves as the initial bridge between strangers, easing into more significant discussions. The key to effective small talk is to find common ground quickly, whether it's discussing a recent industry development, a mutual connection, or even a shared interest outside of work, like a hobby or favorite book. These light conversations can make the networking experience more enjoyable and less daunting, opening doors to deeper exchanges.

Public speaking is another invaluable skill, especially in larger networking settings such as conferences or group meetings. The ability to speak confidently and clearly about your work can position you as a knowledgeable professional in your field, attracting potential collaborators or mentors. To develop this skill, consider joining groups like Toastmasters or taking public speaking courses that offer a safe space to practice and receive constructive feedback.

Modern networking extends beyond face-to-face interactions thanks to the proliferation of digital platforms. LinkedIn, for instance, is a powerhouse for professional networking, allowing you to connect with peers worldwide. To use LinkedIn effectively, ensure your profile is up-to-date and reflects your professional achievements and aspirations. Engage with your network by sharing relevant articles, commenting on posts, and participating in discussions. This ongoing engagement keeps you visible and relevant within your network.

Industry-specific forums and online groups also offer more targeted networking opportunities. Participating in these forums allows you to share your expertise and learn from others facing similar professional challenges. When engaging on these platforms, provide value through thoughtful comments or by sharing resources, which can help you build a reputation as a helpful and knowledgeable professional.

Tailoring your networking strategies to fit your personality is crucial for authentic and sustainable connections. If you are an introvert, you might prefer one-on-one meetings or small group gatherings rather than large networking events. In such cases, focus on building deeper connections with fewer people, which can be just as valuable as having a wide network. For extroverts, larger networking events might be more enjoyable and productive. Regardless of your personality type, finding networking styles and settings that feel natural and effective for you is key.

By embracing these networking strategies and developing essential social skills, you transform networking from a mere professional necessity into a rich community, support, and opportunity source. This proactive approach enriches your professional life and guards against the isolation that can creep into our increasingly digital and remote working environments. As you continue to expand and engage with your network, observe how these connections enrich your professional journey, offering new paths for growth, collaboration, and personal fulfillment.

5.6 Family Dynamics and Burnout: Finding Harmony

In the realm of personal relationships, the family holds a unique and powerful influence over our well-being and stress levels. As societal expectations evolve, a family's traditional and modern roles can sometimes clash or blend in ways that either alleviate or exacerbate stress. Understanding these dynamics is crucial in managing and preventing family-related stress from spiraling into burnout. Each family member may play different roles, influenced by factors such as culture, personal beliefs, and economic conditions, and these roles often come with implicit expectations that can either support or strain individual members.

The stress arising from family responsibilities is often compounded by unspoken expectations. For instance, a working parent may still find themselves disproportionately responsible for home care, or adult children might feel pressure to support aging parents financially. These roles, especially if chosen by default rather than desire, can lead to significant stress. A clear understanding and open discussion of these roles within the family can prevent misunderstandings and unequal distribution of responsibilities, which are common sources of stress and potential burnout. It is beneficial for families to regularly discuss and realign their expectations of each other, considering the changing dynamics of life stages, careers, and personal growth.

Enhancing family communication and cooperation starts with establishing a culture of openness and respect. Family meetings can be structured to discuss everyone's needs, challenges, and expectations. During these discussions, encourage all family members to express their thoughts and feelings openly without fear of judgment. This practice helps clarify roles and expectations and strengthens emotional connections, making it easier for us to support each other during stressful times. Techniques such as active listening, where each person pays full attention to the speaker and refrains from interrupting or preparing a response while the other is speaking, can greatly enhance the quality of these interactions. Additionally, using "I" statements helps in expressing personal feelings without blaming others, which is crucial in maintaining a constructive and supportive dialogue.

Balancing family responsibilities with personal self-care is another critical area that requires careful attention. Recognizing that your well-being is foundational to your ability to care for others effectively is essential. This balance can be achieved by setting aside time for self-care activities that rejuvenate your mind and body, such as exercise, hobbies, or simply quiet time alone. Communicate the importance of this personal time to your family, explaining how these activities help you recharge and maintain your health. Moreover, delegating responsibilities among family members can help distribute the workload more evenly, allowing everyone some breathing room. For instance, involving children in age-appropriate household chores can teach them responsibility and teamwork while easing the burden on parents.

Post-intervention, the transformation in family dynamics can be profound, as illustrated by several case studies. One notable example involves a family where both parents were high-achieving professionals. They found themselves facing burnout due to unbalanced work and family commitments. Through family counseling, they learned to communicate their individual needs more effectively and reallocated household and parenting duties in a way that honored both parents' careers and personal time. This intervention led to a significant reduction in stress and a more harmonious home environment. Another case involved a multi-generational family struggling with boundaries and privacy issues. By establishing clear rules about shared spaces and private times and through regular family meetings to discuss each person's needs, the family experienced improved relationships and a decrease in collective stress.

These real-life examples underscore the effectiveness of proactive communication, role clarification, and self-care prioritization in enhancing family dynamics and reducing stress. By adopting these strategies, families can create a supportive environment that not only withstands the challenges of modern living but also fosters individual and collective well-being.

As we close this chapter on enhancing relationships and social connections, the overarching message is clear: relationships, whether familial, professional, or social, play a pivotal role in our mental and emotional health. The strategies discussed across these sections provide a blueprint for nurturing these connections, ensuring they serve as sources of strength and support rather than stress. In the upcoming chapter, we will explore lifestyle adjustments that further support stress management and burnout prevention, providing you with additional tools to maintain your well-being comprehensively and holistically.

SIX

Lifestyle Adjustments for Preventing Burnout

Imagine you are trying to navigate through a dense fog. Your visibility is compromised, your senses are heightened, and every step forward is taken with cautious uncertainty. Now consider that this fog is not around you but rather within you. This is what living with chronic sleep deprivation can feel like—an obscure haze through which daily life becomes a challenging and exhausting journey. Sleep, or the lack thereof, plays a monumental role in your overall well-being and stress management, and understanding this relationship is crucial in preventing and recovering from burnout.

6.1 The Impact of Sleep on Well-Being and Stress

The Science of Sleep and Stress

Sleep is not merely a passive state of rest but a dynamic process that affects various physiological systems, including the brain's ability to manage stress. When you sleep, your body goes through multiple cycles of REM (Rapid Eye Movement) and NREM (Non-Rapid Eye Movement) sleep. Each cycle helps to repair and rejuvenate the body and mind. Specifically, NREM sleep, which constitutes about 75% of your sleep cycle, is crucial for physical recovery, including tissue repair and the immune system's strengthening. REM sleep, on the other hand, plays a critical role in emotional and cognitive processing, helping to consolidate memories and regulate emotions.

Lack of adequate sleep disrupts these cycles and can increase cortisol, the body's main stress hormone. Elevated cortisol levels heighten your body's stress response and inhibit your ability to relax and recover, creating a vicious cycle of stress and sleeplessness. This disruption can also impair your prefrontal cortex, an area of the brain responsible for decision-making, emotional regulation, and focused attention, further exacerbating feelings of frustration and anxiety.

Guidelines for Healthy Sleep Hygiene

Establishing a routine that promotes good sleep hygiene is essential to combat the effects of sleep deprivation. Here are some practical tips to enhance your sleep quality:

- Establish a Regular Sleep Schedule: Go to bed and wake up at the same time every day, even on weekends. Consistency reinforces your body's sleep-wake cycle.

- Create a Restful Environment: Make sure your bedroom is conducive to sleeping. It should be cool, quiet, and dark. Invest in good quality bedding, and consider using blackout curtains or eye masks to block light.
- Wind Down Before Bed: Develop a relaxing bedtime routine to signal to your body that it's time to wind down. This could include reading, taking a warm bath, or meditating.
- Limit Stimulants: Avoid caffeine and nicotine close to bedtime, as they can interfere with your ability to fall asleep. Also, be wary of heavy meals and alcohol, which can disrupt sleep later at night.

Consequences of Sleep Deprivation

Chronic sleep deprivation can lead to severe physical and mental health issues. Physically, it increases the risk of various conditions such as heart disease, diabetes, and obesity. Mentally, it leads to impaired cognitive function, reduced attention span, and decreased emotional stability. In the context of burnout, these effects can be particularly detrimental, exacerbating feelings of inefficacy, cynicism, and exhaustion.

Tools for Better Sleep

To help monitor and improve your sleep patterns, consider utilizing technology designed for sleep enhancement:

- Sleep Trackers: Devices like Fitbit or apps such as Sleep Cycle can monitor your sleep patterns, providing insights into the quality and quantity of your sleep. They can help identify any disturbances or irregularities in your sleep that you may need to address.
- Relaxation Apps: Apps such as Calm or Headspace offer guided meditations and stories to help you relax and prepare for sleep.

Understanding the critical role sleep plays in stress management and overall health and implementing practices that encourage good sleep hygiene can significantly improve your resilience against burnout. Making sleep a priority is not just about preventing fatigue; it's about fostering a foundation of well-being that supports all aspects of your life, allowing you to function personally and professionally at your best.

6.2 Dietary Choices to Boost Energy and Mood

In the bustling rhythm of daily life, the role of diet often plays a critical backdrop to how you feel, both physically and emotionally. It's not just about the foods you eat but understanding the essential nutrients that sustain your energy and stabilize your mood. Complex carbohydrates, lean proteins, and healthy fats form the triad that should anchor your dietary choices. Complex carbohydrates in foods like whole grains, legumes, and vegetables are crucial as they provide a steady release of glucose into your bloodstream, offering a sustained energy supply without the spikes associated with simple sugars. Lean proteins, such as chicken, fish, and tofu, are vital for their role in neurotransmitter function, which can influence your mood and stress levels. Foods rich in healthy fats, like avocados, nuts, and seeds, contribute to brain health and are integral in managing mood fluctuations.

Hydration also plays a pivotal role in maintaining optimal mental and physical health. It's not just about quenching thirst—adequate hydration affects your energy levels and cognitive functions. Water facilitates the chemical reactions in your body, including energy production and signal transmission in your nervous system. Guidelines suggest aiming for about 2 liters of water a day, but this can vary based on your activity level and environmental conditions. To integrate this into your routine, consider starting your day with a glass of water and keeping a reusable water bottle handy throughout the day. This helps meet your hydration needs and is a constant reminder to drink water regularly.

Incorporating healthy eating into a hectic schedule might seem daunting, but with a bit of planning, it can seamlessly fit into your busy lifestyle. Meal prepping is a powerful strategy that involves preparing meals or components of meals ahead of time. Dedicate a few hours over the weekend to batch-cook meals or prepare ingredients like chopped vegetables and cooked grains that can be quickly assembled into healthy dishes throughout the week. This saves time and ensures that you have nutritious meals on hand, reducing the temptation to opt for less healthy, convenience foods. For snacks, choose options that combine complex carbohydrates with protein, such as apple slices with peanut butter or yogurt with berries, which can provide a quick and satisfying energy boost.

Avoiding dietary pitfalls is crucial in maintaining consistent energy levels and a stable mood. High sugar intake, for example, can lead to quick spikes and subsequent crashes in blood sugar levels, which can induce feelings of fatigue and irritability. Similarly, irregular eating patterns can disrupt your body's natural rhythms, leading to fluctuations in energy and mood. To avoid these pitfalls, strive to consume balanced meals at regular intervals. This not only helps in regulating your body's physiological processes but also aids in sustaining your focus and energy throughout the day.

Understanding and implementing these dietary principles can significantly influence your energy levels and mood, which are essential in managing stress and preventing burnout. Making informed choices about what you eat, staying hydrated, planning your meals, and avoiding dietary traps form a comprehensive approach to sustaining both your physical vitality and emotional stability. As you continue to explore the potent role of nutrition in your health, remember that these simple changes can have a profound impact on your overall well-being, enabling you to tackle your daily challenges with renewed vigor and a balanced state of mind.

6.3 The Importance of Leisure and Downtime

In the relentless pursuit of productivity and success, it's alarmingly easy to sideline leisure and downtime—those golden pockets of the day dedicated purely to relaxation and personal enjoyment. Yet, it's precisely these moments that wield the power to rejuvenate our minds, soothe our emotions, and replenish our energy reserves. Engaging in leisure activities is not merely an escape from the demands of daily life but a vital component of mental health management. By stepping away from work-related tasks and immersing ourselves in activities that bring us joy, we initiate a mental and emotional recovery process that is essential in counteracting the symptoms of burnout. This restoration is not just about alleviating immediate stress but about building a reservoir of calm and resilience that can buffer against future stressors.

Leisure activities come in many forms and need not be time-consuming or expensive. The key is to find activities that resonate with your interests and provide a sense of satisfaction or relaxation. For some, this might mean engaging in physical activities like hiking or yoga, which provide a mental break and enhance physical health. Others may find solace in creative pursuits such as painting, writing, or playing a musical instrument, which can serve as expressive outlets and sources of personal fulfillment. Even simpler activities like reading a book, watching a favorite show, or gardening can serve as effective forms of leisure. The variety of options means that there is something for everyone, and integrating these activities into your regular schedule can significantly enhance your quality of life.

Balancing productivity with leisure is a delicate art that requires conscious planning and prioritization. It's crucial to recognize that time spent in leisure is not time wasted but rather an investment in your overall well-being. To integrate leisure effectively, begin by examining your current schedule. Identify blocks of time that are typically spent in low-value activities or unproductive downtime, such as scrolling through social media or watching unfulfilling television.

Consider reallocating some of this time to more rewarding leisure activities. Planning leisure activities in advance can also help; just as you would schedule a meeting or a doctor's appointment, try scheduling a regular slot for leisure in your daily or weekly planner. This ensures that you reserve time for relaxation and helps build a routine that equally prioritizes work and leisure.

The importance of making leisure a non-negotiable part of your routine cannot be overstated. In the same way that we understand the necessity of daily practices like eating and sleeping for our physical health, we must acknowledge leisure as crucial for our mental health. To cultivate this mindset, start by setting small, achievable goals for incorporating leisure into your life. This could be as simple as dedicating thirty minutes to a leisure activity of your choice each day. Gradually, as you begin to experience the benefits—such as reduced stress, improved mood, and increased energy—you may find it natural to extend or diversify the time you dedicate to leisure activities. Remember, the goal is to build a sustainable balance that supports both your productivity and your well-being, allowing you to function optimally in all areas of your life.

By embracing the importance of leisure and downtime, you take a crucial step towards safeguarding your mental health and enhancing your life quality. Leisure activities provide a necessary counterbalance to work pressures, offering a space for recovery and enjoyment essential for long-term well-being. As you continue to explore and integrate these practices, you'll likely discover that they enrich your days and empower you to handle life's challenges with greater resilience and perspective. This realization underscores the profound impact of well-managed leisure time on your overall health and happiness, making it a vital component of a balanced, fulfilling life.

6.4 Creating a Restorative Home Environment

The spaces we inhabit play a pivotal role in influencing our emotional and psychological well-being. Your home, which should be a sanctuary from the stresses of the outside world, can significantly impact your ability to relax and rejuvenate. When your living environment is harmoniously arranged to promote relaxation, it can vastly reduce stress levels and mitigate the risk of burnout. Conversely, a chaotic or discomforting home environment can exacerbate stress, leaving you more vulnerable to feeling overwhelmed. Thus, the importance of crafting a supportive living space cannot be overstated, especially for those seeking to cultivate a lifestyle resilient against burnout.

Creating a calming home environment begins with your living space's intentional design and organization. Start with decluttering, a simple yet effective step towards reducing anxiety and promoting ease of mind. Clutter is not just physically obstructive; it can be mentally overwhelming, constantly signaling to your brain that there's always more to be done. Keeping your living space tidy and organized eliminates these stress triggers, creating a more peaceful and inviting environment. Consider adopting minimalist principles, which emphasize keeping only what is necessary and meaningful to help maintain a clutter-free home.

The choice of color scheme in your home also plays a crucial role in creating a calming atmosphere. Soft, neutral colors like light blues, greens, and grays are known for their soothing effects on the mind and can help create a tranquil space conducive to relaxation. These colors mimic elements of nature and the outdoors, which are inherently calming and restorative. If repainting walls isn't an option, incorporating these colors through accents such as throw pillows, curtains, or rugs can also be effective.

Incorporating natural elements into your home decor can further enhance the calming quality of your environment. Houseplants, for instance, add a touch of vitality and freshness to your space and improve air quality, which can positively affect your mood and health. The act of caring for plants can also be a soothing activity, offering a pleasant distraction from the pressures of daily life. Additionally, natural materials such as wooden furniture, stone decorations, or water features can create a sense of grounding and connection to the natural world, reinforcing a peaceful atmosphere.

Maintaining distinct areas for work and relaxation is crucial for those who work from home. Blurring these boundaries can lead to a constant mental association of home with work stress, making it difficult to switch off and fully relax. Designate a specific area of your home, even if it's just a particular desk or corner, exclusively for work-related activities. Equally, have areas set aside for relaxation, such as a cozy reading nook or a comfortable spot with soft lighting and cushions for meditation or listening to music. This physical separation helps mentally compartmentalize your activities, enabling you to detach from work and fully relax when needed.

The Role of Sensory Elements in Enhancing Calm

The influence of sensory elements in shaping the atmosphere of your home is profound and often underestimated. These elements—scents, textures, and sounds—can directly impact your mood and stress levels by evoking relaxation or, if not carefully curated, contributing to sensory overload. Integrating calming sensory experiences into your home environment can significantly enhance its restorative effects.

Scents, for instance, have a powerful link to emotional and memory centers in the brain. Incorporating soothing scents through candles, essential oils, or incense can create a tranquil ambiance. Lavender, chamomile, and sandalwood are popular for their calming properties and can be particularly beneficial in spaces designated for relaxation or sleep. On the other hand, peppermint and citrus scents can be energizing and are ideal for workspaces to help maintain focus and alertness.

The textures in your home also contribute to its overall feel and comfort. Soft, plush textures invite relaxation and provide physical comfort, which can ease stress. Consider soft throw blankets, cushy pillows, or a comfortable armchair upholstered in a gentle fabric. These elements enhance the aesthetic appeal of your home and invite you to relax and indulge in comfort, promoting a sense of well-being.

Sound is another critical sensory element. In many urban environments, the constant background noise of traffic, construction, or even general city bustle can be subtly stressful. Counteracting this noise with soothing sounds can help in creating a more restorative home environment. Sound machines that emulate natural noises like rainfall, ocean waves, or forest sounds can mask unpleasant background noise and foster relaxation. Alternatively, soft, instrumental music or even the strategic placement of wind chimes can fill your home with soothing sounds that encourage relaxation and mental decompression.

By thoughtfully curating these sensory elements, you transform your home into a truly restorative environment that shelters your body and supports your mental and emotional health. This deliberate crafting of your living space is not merely about aesthetic appeal but about creating a sanctuary that actively contributes to your well-being, helping stave off the mental and physical exhaustion characteristic of burnout. As you refine and adapt your living space, you'll find that these small changes can profoundly impact your daily life, enhancing your ability to relax, recharge, and resist the pressures that lead to burnout.

6.5 Financial Stress and Burnout: Managing Economic Anxiety

The specter of financial stress looms large in the lives of many, weaving a complex web of anxiety that can seep into both personal and professional realms. The worry over finances is not merely about numbers and budgets; it's deeply intertwined with our sense of security and stability. When financial stress becomes a persistent shadow, it can catalyze a cascade of psychological pressures that may culminate in burnout. This type of stress is insidious because it affects your immediate state of mind and impairs your ability to focus, make decisions, and perform effectively at work. The fear of not meeting financial obligations or the constant struggle to manage debt can keep you in a state of heightened anxiety, contributing to sleep disturbances, irritability, and a pervasive sense of hopelessness, all hallmark symptoms of burnout.

Addressing financial stress proactively involves adopting basic financial planning strategies that can provide a more effective framework for managing your finances. Budgeting is the cornerstone of personal financial management. It involves tracking your income and expenses to understand where your money goes each month. Start by listing your essential expenses, such as rent, utilities, groceries, and transportation. Then, factor in discretionary spending and savings. The goal is to ensure that your spending does not exceed your income and that you are setting aside money for future needs, including an emergency fund. Tools like budgeting apps or spreadsheets can simplify this process by visually representing your finances and helping you stay on track.

Debt management is another crucial strategy in alleviating financial stress. If you find yourself dealing with high levels of debt, prioritize paying off high-interest debts first, such as credit card debts, as they are the most costly. Consider strategies like debt consolidation or refinancing to lower interest rates and reduce monthly payments. For long-term debts like student loans or mortgages, ensure that you understand the terms and explore options for more manageable repayment plans if necessary. It's also wise to avoid taking on new debt unless absolutely essential, focusing instead on paying down existing obligations.

Building an emergency savings fund can significantly reduce financial stress by providing a buffer to handle unexpected expenses or income disruptions without resorting to credit. Aim to save at least three to six months' worth of living expenses. Start small if necessary, and gradually build this fund over time. Automated savings plans, where a portion of your paycheck is directly transferred to a savings account, can facilitate this process by making saving a regular, effortless habit.

For more personalized guidance in managing finances, consider seeking advice from a financial advisor. These professionals can offer customized strategies based on your individual financial situation, goals, and challenges. Additionally, many community programs offer free or low-cost financial counseling services that can provide valuable advice on budgeting, debt management, and saving. Online resources, such as financial education websites and tools, can offer insights and strategies to improve financial literacy and management skills.

Taking proactive steps to manage your finances effectively is crucial not just for your economic well-being but also for your overall mental health. By implementing sound financial practices, you not only mitigate the stress associated with money management but also empower yourself to make informed decisions that can enhance your financial stability and reduce the risk of burnout. Remember, financial health is an integral part of your total well-being; nurturing it proactively can lead to a more balanced and fulfilling life.

6.6 The Benefits of Routine Health Check-Ups

In the same way you would regularly service your car to prevent breakdowns, routine health check-ups are essential maintenance for your body and mind, ensuring everything is functioning optimally. These check-ups are vital not only for catching potential health issues early but also for managing stress effectively. Regular health evaluations provide a clear picture of how your body is coping with stress, allowing you to make informed decisions about necessary changes to your lifestyle or work habits. For example, discovering that you have high blood pressure could be a signal that your current methods of stress management are insufficient, prompting you to explore additional strategies such as meditation or counseling.

Routine health screenings are tailored to various stages of life and consider factors such as age, gender, family history, and lifestyle. For adults, these screenings typically include blood pressure checks, cholesterol levels, diabetes screening, and assessments for cardiovascular health. Women may have additional screenings such as mammograms and cervical cancer screenings, while men might be recommended for prostate cancer screenings. Keeping up with these recommended screenings is crucial, as it allows you to take preventive measures against potential health issues that can exacerbate stress and lead to burnout.

Incorporating mental health assessments into your routine check-ups is an effective way to monitor your psychological well-being. Just as physical ailments can impair your ability to perform daily tasks, mental health issues can significantly impact your quality of life and stress levels. Regular discussions with your healthcare provider about your mental state can help in identifying signs of stress, anxiety, or depression early. It also serves to normalize mental health care, integrating it into your overall health management strategy. These assessments can guide your doctor in recommending interventions or adjustments to your stress management techniques, ensuring they are effective and tailored to your needs.

Building a consistent and open relationship with your healthcare provider is another foundational element of effective health management. When you have a strong rapport with your doctor, you're more likely to be honest about your symptoms and concerns, which leads to more personalized and effective care. This relationship is built over time through regular interactions and open communication. Make it a point to be prepared for your appointments with notes on any symptoms or concerns, and don't hesitate to ask questions about your health and treatments. Remember, a collaborative relationship with your healthcare provider empowers you to take charge of your health, which is crucial in managing stress and preventing burnout.

By understanding and utilizing the benefits of routine health check-ups, you place yourself in a proactive position to manage your health effectively. This proactive approach helps catch and address issues before they escalate and supports your overall strategy for stress management and burnout prevention. As you continue to navigate life, remember that these regular health assessments are your allies, providing you with the insights and support needed to maintain your physical and mental well-being.

As this chapter on lifestyle adjustments for preventing burnout concludes, we reflect on the profound impact of proactive health management, balanced nutrition, adequate sleep, financial stability, and personal leisure on our overall quality of life. Each element plays a critical role in not just addressing burnout symptoms but crafting a life rich in well-being and satisfaction. The subsequent chapters will continue exploring additional strategies and insights that will equip you to maintain this balance, ensuring that you thrive in all facets of life.

SEVEN

Special Considerations and Populations

I n the labyrinth of modern professions, few carry the emotional and physical toll experienced by healthcare professionals. Every day, these dedicated individuals step into roles that demand not just their expertise and attention but also a piece of their compassion and emotional resilience. The stakes are exceptionally high—dealing not with figures on a spreadsheet but with human lives. Within this high-stakes arena, understanding and addressing the unique facets of burnout in healthcare professionals is not just beneficial; it's imperative. As we navigate through this exploration, remember that the strategies and insights offered are tailored to fortify your resilience and enhance your capacity to care for others without sacrificing your well-being.

7.1 Burnout in Healthcare Professionals: A Closer Look

Understanding the Unique Stressors

Healthcare professionals face a triad of intense stressors: prolonged hours, the emotional weight of patient care, and the critical nature of their work outcomes. The long hours are not merely a matter of fatigue; they disrupt the natural rhythms of rest and personal life, creating a cascade of stress that extends beyond the individual to affect their families and social lives. Moreover, the emotional labor involved in patient care is profound. Healthcare workers extend immense emotional energy daily, empathizing with patients who are often distressed, fearful, and in pain. This continuous expenditure of emotional energy can lead to what is known as compassion fatigue, a state of emotional exhaustion that closely mirrors and contributes to burnout.

The pressure of producing favorable medical outcomes cannot be overstated. Often, the decisions made by healthcare workers can have life-altering consequences for their patients. This high-stakes environment, where the line between success and failure often hangs on quick decision-making and precision, significantly amplifies stress, pushing many toward burnout.

Strategies for Emotional Detachment

Learning to manage emotional involvement without compromising compassionate care is crucial to mitigating the risk of emotional exhaustion. Techniques such as setting emotional boundaries and practicing self-awareness can be highly effective. Setting boundaries involves recognizing the limit to the emotional energy you can invest in patients while maintaining professional empathy. On the other hand, self-awareness entails understanding your emotional triggers and acknowledging when your resources are depleted, prompting you to step back and replenish.

A practical approach to fostering emotional detachment is through reflective practice and supervision. Healthcare professionals can discuss difficult cases with peers or supervisors to gain insights and emotional support without breaching patient confidentiality. This practice provides a safety valve for emotional pressure and contributes to professional development and better patient care.

Peer Support Systems

The role of peer support systems in mitigating burnout cannot be underestimated. These systems provide a network of understanding and empathy for individuals who face similar challenges and stressors. Formal support systems such as mentoring programs, support groups, and team debriefings can offer spaces where healthcare professionals can share experiences, offer solutions, and support each other emotionally and practically. These interactions alleviate feelings of isolation and foster a sense of community and shared purpose, which is vital in a field as demanding as healthcare.

Mindfulness and Resilience Training

To fortify healthcare professionals against the challenges of their roles, targeted programs that focus on building resilience and practicing mindfulness are essential. These programs teach techniques to manage stress, regulate emotions, and maintain a present-focused orientation despite the chaotic environment. Mindfulness training, in particular, helps develop a non-judgmental awareness of the present moment, enhances emotional regulation, and decreases reactivity to stressful situations. Hospitals and healthcare institutions are increasingly recognizing these programs' value and integrating them into their professional development offerings.

Programs like Mindfulness-Based Stress Reduction (MBSR) and resilience workshops provide structured approaches to developing these skills. These programs often include practices such as guided meditations, breathing exercises, and group discussions that help individuals learn to center themselves and maintain calmness in the face of daily pressures.

As we continue to explore the dimensions of burnout across various professions, it's clear that the challenges faced by healthcare professionals are uniquely demanding. However, it is possible to manage these stressors effectively with the right strategies and support. By prioritizing emotional detachment techniques, fostering strong peer support networks, and committing to regular mindfulness and resilience training, healthcare professionals can protect their well-being and enhance their capacity to provide compassionate and effective care.

7.2 Entrepreneurs and Burnout: Balancing Passion and Health

The entrepreneurial spirit is fueled by a relentless pursuit of innovation and success, traits that, while admirable, often lead individuals down a path where passion collides with the risk of burnout. Entrepreneurs typically immerse themselves deeply in their ventures, driven by a personal commitment that blurs the boundaries between work and life. This deep involvement, though powerful, can make it difficult for entrepreneurs to recognize the early signs of burnout. Symptoms such as persistent fatigue, irritability, and a gradual decrease in satisfaction and effectiveness may be dismissed as mere side effects of a busy season or justified in the name of ambition. However, acknowledging these early warnings is crucial. It allows for the implementation of preventative strategies that safeguard your health and ensure your business's sustainability and growth.

One fundamental strategy in preventing burnout is setting realistic goals and expectations. The entrepreneurial journey is often romanticized as a rapid rise to success, but the reality is typically marked by setbacks and slow progress. By setting achievable goals, you align your day-to-day activities with a more accurate vision of success that acknowledges and prepares for challenges. This approach reduces frustration and discouragement, which are often precipitated by unmet expectations based on overly ambitious or poorly defined goals. Maintaining realistic expectations involves continuous learning and adapting, enhancing your business acumen and keeping you grounded in your venture's practical aspects.

Delegation plays a pivotal role in managing the demands of entrepreneurship. Many entrepreneurs fall into the trap of believing they must handle every aspect of their business personally. This misconception can lead to overwhelming stress and burnout. Effective delegation involves identifying tasks that do not require your direct input and entrusting them to reliable team members or outsourcing them. This practice frees up your time for tasks that necessitate your unique skills, empowers your team, and promotes a collaborative work environment. Moreover, delegation helps maintain your mental health by preventing task saturation, which can cloud decision-making and stifle creativity.

Building a supportive network is another crucial element in the entrepreneurial framework against burnout. This network should include mentors who provide guidance based on their experiences, peers who offer relatable insights and mutual support, and professionals like business coaches or mental health experts who can offer specialized advice. Engaging with this network helps you gain perspective, encouraging you to step back and evaluate both your personal well-being and business health through various lenses. These relationships also provide a safety net, offering advice and support when you face challenges. Additionally, this network serves as a sounding board for your ideas and concerns, helping you refine your strategies and avoid potential pitfalls.

As you continue to navigate the complexities of entrepreneurship, remember that your health and well-being are integral to your success. Recognizing the signs of burnout, setting realistic goals, delegating effectively, and cultivating a supportive network are not just strategies for business efficiency but practices that sustain your passion and vitality. By integrating these strategies into your daily operations, you create a balanced approach to entrepreneurship that respects your personal health and professional ambitions. This balanced approach enhances your capacity to lead and ensures that your journey in entrepreneurship is sustainable and rewarding, marked by growth and innovation that do not come at the expense of your well-being.

7.3 Parents Managing Burnout: Tips for Moms and Dads

Parenting, while deeply rewarding, inherently involves a complex juggling act that can often lead to stress and burnout if not managed carefully. Balancing the 24/7 demands of childcare with personal needs requires time management, emotional intelligence, and proactive strategies to ensure your well-being and that of your family. The key is to find harmony between meeting your children's needs and attending to your own personal health and happiness. One effective approach is to integrate self-care into your daily routine. This might mean setting aside specific times during the day for activities that rejuvenate you, such as reading, exercising, or engaging in a hobby. It's also beneficial to establish routines involving your children in activities that allow you to unwind together, such as walking or cycling, providing physical activity and valuable bonding time.

Communication within the family unit plays a pivotal role in managing expectations and sharing responsibilities, which are crucial for reducing stress for all involved. It's important for partners to have open and honest discussions about their feelings, expectations, and the practicalities of parenting. This can involve negotiating who does what chores or deciding on parenting techniques. For single parents, seeking support from extended family or friends to share the caregiving load is vital. Regular family meetings can be a useful forum for discussing issues and making decisions together as a family. These meetings encourage children to express their needs and understand the dynamics of family responsibilities, fostering a cooperative spirit.

Community resources play a significant role in providing support and relief to parents. Engaging with local parenting groups offers an opportunity to connect with others who are facing similar challenges. These groups often provide emotional support as well as practical advice and can be a great source of friendship and understanding. Family counseling services can also be beneficial, especially when dealing with specific challenges that affect family dynamics, such as behavioral issues with children or communication problems between partners. Additionally, childcare services, even for a few hours a week, can provide essential breaks for parents, allowing them some personal time to recharge or attend to other responsibilities.

Incorporating stress-relieving activities into family life is beneficial for reducing parental stress and enhancing the family's overall emotional well-being. Activities that focus on relaxation and enjoyment can help mitigate the daily pressures of family life. For instance, planning regular family outings such as picnics in the park, visits to a museum, or short hikes can provide a change of scenery and a break from routine, which can be refreshing for both parents and children. Engaging in creative activities together, like arts and crafts or baking, can also be therapeutic, offering a fun and productive way to spend time together while diverting from everyday stressors.

By adopting these strategies, parents can better manage parenting demands while maintaining their health and well-being. This balanced approach helps foster a nurturing environment that supports children's and parents' growth and happiness. Remember, the goal is not to perfect the balancing act but rather to find ways to make it more enjoyable and less stressful for the whole family. As you continue to explore and implement these strategies, observe the positive changes in your family dynamics and your sense of well-being, knowing that each step you take builds a stronger, happier family foundation.

7.4 Students and Young Professionals: Early Intervention

The pressures of academic achievements and professional milestones can be overwhelming in the vibrant yet often tumultuous stages of student life and early career development. The transition from the structured environment of education to the dynamic world of professional work often brings unanticipated challenges that can contribute to stress and burnout. Recognizing the critical need for early intervention, educational institutions and workplaces are increasingly advocating for the integration of stress management and mental health programs. These programs serve as essential resources, providing students and young professionals with the tools and knowledge to navigate stress effectively. By introducing stress management techniques through workshops, seminars, and accessible counseling services, these institutions play a pivotal role in fostering a supportive environment that encourages mental wellness from the outset.

Implementing comprehensive career counseling services that emphasize realistic goal-setting is another cornerstone in supporting young professionals. Career counselors can provide invaluable guidance by helping individuals set achievable career goals that align with their skills, interests, and values, thus preventing the common pitfall of chasing ill-fitted or overly ambitious career paths that lead to frustration and burnout. These services should also focus on educating young professionals about the normalcy of career challenges and the importance of flexibility and resilience. Through regular counseling sessions, career development workshops, and networking events, young professionals can better understand the career landscape, which empowers them to make informed decisions and set realistic expectations for their career progression.

Furthermore, the concept of building a balanced lifestyle is essential in this early phase of adult life. It's crucial for students and young professionals to learn how to maintain a healthy equilibrium between work, study, social activities, and personal health. Educational programs and employers can facilitate this by promoting time management skills, providing physical and mental health resources, and encouraging participation in social and extracurricular activities. For instance, universities and workplaces can offer access to fitness centers, mental health workshops, and social clubs, which help individuals build routines that encompass all aspects of a healthy lifestyle. Additionally, fostering environments where young adults feel comfortable discussing their work-life balance concerns can lead to more personalized support and adjustment in academic or work expectations.

Mentorship is another powerful tool in the arsenal against burnout among students and young professionals. Having access to a mentor who can offer guidance, share experiences, and provide emotional and professional support is invaluable. These mentors act as role models and advisors, helping mentees navigate the complexities of their new roles and responsibilities while offering strategies to manage stress. Mentorship programs can be formal, with mentors assigned through educational programs or professional organizations, or informal, developed through personal or professional connections. By participating in these relationships, young individuals gain confidence, receive encouragement, and learn coping strategies that are crucial for managing stress and preventing burnout.

By integrating these proactive strategies—stress management education, realistic career planning, lifestyle balance, and mentorship—into the fabric of educational and professional development programs, we can equip students and young professionals with the resilience and skills needed to thrive in their personal and professional lives. This early intervention enhances individual well-being and contributes to a healthier, more productive educational and professional environment. As we continue to explore and implement these strategies, the journey of education and early career development can transform into a more supportive and engaging experience marked by growth, learning, and well-being.

7.5 Burnout in the Non-profit Sector: Coping Strategies

Working in the non-profit sector often involves a high-emotion environment, where daily interactions may include dealing with individuals or communities in vulnerable situations. This exposure, while part of the fulfilling aspect of non-profit work, carries with it a unique set of emotional challenges. The relentless pursuit of mission-driven goals, often under significant resource constraints, can lead to a unique kind of stress known as 'mission stress', characterized by a deep sense of responsibility and urgency to make a difference. This emotional investment can be both a blessing and a burden, providing motivation and satisfaction on one hand but also leading to emotional exhaustion if not managed properly.

The emotional toll of working with underprivileged or distressed populations can be mitigated through specific coping strategies that focus on emotional management. One effective approach is the practice of compartmentalization—learning to separate the emotional aspects of work from personal life. This does not mean becoming indifferent but rather developing the ability to distance oneself emotionally when necessary to preserve personal well-being. Techniques such as reflective journaling or debriefing sessions with colleagues can also provide outlets for expressing and processing emotions in a healthy manner, helping to prevent the accumulation of stress.

Moreover, the nature of non-profit work often involves funding and job security uncertainty. This financial instability can add a layer of stress, impacting not just the operational capacities of the organization but also the personal lives of its employees. To navigate these challenges, it is crucial to develop a proactive approach to financial planning at the organizational and personal levels. Organizations can strive to create more diversified funding streams to reduce dependency on single sources, while individuals should be encouraged to manage personal finances with an eye toward stability, such as maintaining a savings buffer or exploring secondary income options to mitigate financial stress.

Creating a supportive organizational culture is another critical strategy for coping with burnout in the non-profit sector. This involves fostering an environment where staff feel valued, supported, and understood. Leaders in non-profit organizations should prioritize regular check-ins with staff to gauge stress levels and provide support where needed. Developing formal support structures such as peer-mentoring programs, mental health days, and access to professional counseling can also significantly improve staff morale and mental health. Moreover, promoting a culture that values transparency and open communication can help address potential issues before they escalate into serious problems, ensuring that employees feel their voices are heard and that their contributions are recognized.

Finally, the importance of self-care and boundary setting cannot be overstated in emotionally demanding work environments. Non-profit professionals must be equipped with the tools and knowledge to establish and maintain healthy boundaries between work and personal life. This might include setting clear work-hour limits, learning to say no when workload demands exceed capacity, and developing personal rituals that help transition from work to personal time, such as a short walk after work or a designated quiet hour before bedtime. Additionally, regular engagement in self-care activities that promote physical and mental health, such as exercise, hobbies, and social activities, is essential for replenishing the energy and emotional resilience needed to continue performing effectively in one's role.

Developing robust coping strategies is essential for sustainability and effectiveness in non-profit work, with high emotional and financial stakes. By integrating these practices into daily routines and organizational policies, non-profit professionals can safeguard their mental health and continue to perform their crucial roles without succumbing to burnout. As we further explore burnout across different sectors, these insights highlight the specific challenges faced by non-profit workers and underscore the universal importance of proactive stress management and organizational support in fostering healthy, productive work environments.

7.6 Creatives and Burnout: Sustaining Inspiration

In the realm of creative work, the pressures of deadlines, criticism, and the inevitable creative blocks can dim the brightest of sparks. For artists, writers, designers, and all who create, these challenges are not merely hurdles but potential triggers that can spiral into burnout. Managing these pressures requires not just resilience but strategic approaches tailored to sustain creativity and maintain mental well-being. It is essential to navigate these stresses with a clear understanding that the health of your creative spirit is as crucial as the projects you undertake.

Creatives often face the daunting task of balancing their passion for creating with the practical aspects of their careers, such as marketing and administrative tasks. These practical tasks, while essential for career success, can often feel like they're encroaching on the time and energy reserved for creative work. To manage this, time management becomes a critical skill. Implementing systems like time-blocking can significantly enhance your productivity by designating specific times for creative work and other times for administrative tasks. This method helps in establishing a routine where creativity can flourish without the looming stress of unchecked emails or unmet marketing needs. Additionally, setting clear and achievable goals for both creative and practical tasks can provide a sense of accomplishment and clarity, reducing feelings of overwhelm and frustration.

Criticism, whether constructive or disparaging, can significantly impact a creative's mindset. Developing a thick skin is often suggested, but cultivating a constructive response to criticism is more important. This involves learning to differentiate between feedback that is useful and that which is not aligned with your vision or growth. Building such discernment allows you to engage with criticism productively, using it to foster growth rather than letting it seed doubt about your abilities or creative worth.

Creative blocks, the bane of any creative's existence, can be particularly disheartening. These periods of seeming inactivity reflect not a lack of talent but a natural part of the creative process. Switching your creative medium or activity is one effective way to navigate these frustrating times. For instance, a writer might take up sketching for a few days, or a painter might explore photography. This provides a break from the routine and can spark creativity in unexpected ways. Additionally, engaging in activities unrelated to your work, such as hiking or cooking, can provide mental relaxation and open new avenues of inspiration.

Building a supportive community with other creatives plays a pivotal role in sustaining inspiration and mitigating feelings of isolation, which are common in creative professions. Networking with peers is not just about building professional connections; it's about creating relationships where ideas, challenges, and successes can be shared openly. Participating in workshops, attending art shows, or joining online forums are excellent ways to connect with like-minded individuals. These interactions can invigorate your creative enthusiasm and provide new perspectives that enrich your own work.

Regularly scheduled creative breaks are essential. Just like any professional needs a vacation to recharge, creatives need time away from their art to rejuvenate their minds and spirits. Planning regular intervals—whether it's a short weekend retreat every few months or designated hours within the week when no work is allowed—can provide much-needed downtime. These breaks are not lapses in productivity but crucial periods that allow for mental and creative renewal, ensuring that you return to your work with renewed vigor and fresh perspectives.

In navigating the landscape of creative work, where the pressure to constantly produce and innovate can be overwhelming, it is crucial to remember that your creative output is deeply tied to your well-being. By implementing strategies to manage the pressures of creative work, balance the demands of your career, and connect with a supportive community, you can maintain a healthy relationship with your creative practice. This ensures your personal well-being and sustains the very inspiration and passion that fuels your work, allowing you to continue creating with joy and fulfillment.

As this chapter on special considerations and populations concludes, we've explored how tailored strategies can help various groups manage their unique challenges, reinforcing the overarching theme that understanding and addressing specific stressors is crucial in preventing burnout. In the next chapter, we will delve into the essential practices that can be adopted universally to foster resilience and well-being, ensuring that individuals from all walks of life can thrive in their personal and professional endeavors.

EIGHT

Ongoing Wellness and Personal Growth

As the sun rises, bringing light to new possibilities and challenges alike, so does the opportunity for personal growth and continuous learning illuminate our lives. Much like the sun's rays breaking through the morning mist, the pursuit of knowledge dispels the fog of routine and complacency that can cloud our mental and emotional landscapes. This chapter is dedicated to exploring how lifelong learning is not just an academic exercise but a vital component of maintaining and enhancing mental health and overall life satisfaction.

8.1 The Role of Continuous Learning in Personal Fulfillment

Link Learning to Mental Health

The human brain is not a static organ but a dynamic entity that thrives on stimulation and challenge. Continuous learning activities activate neural pathways, fostering mental agility and emotional satisfaction. When you learn something new, your brain builds new connections, and this process can be incredibly invigorating and fulfilling. It helps to stave off mental stagnation and provides a sense of achievement and confidence. Moreover, the act of learning can serve as a therapeutic distraction from the stresses of daily life, offering a mental respite that can help prevent the onset of burnout. Whether mastering a new language, understanding a complex concept, or simply discovering a historical fact, each piece of knowledge acquired enriches your mental tapestry, making you more resilient to mental fatigue and ennui.

Incorporate Learning into Everyday Life

Incorporating learning into your daily routine need not be a daunting task reserved for those with ample free time. It can be as simple as modifying your existing habits to include educational elements. For instance, consider the time you spend commuting. This can be transformed into a productive learning session through educational podcasts or audiobooks covering a myriad of topics, from science to self-development. Alternatively, the daily ritual of reading the news can be expanded to include articles from thought leaders or research summaries in fields that interest you. Even the act of cooking dinner can become an educational experience by exploring recipes from different cultures, each offering a lesson in geography, history, and nutrition.

Benefits of Diverse Knowledge Acquisition

Diversifying the subjects you learn about can significantly broaden your perspective, enhancing both personal and professional aspects of your life. Learning about diverse cultures, for example, can increase empathy and communication skills, valuable traits in both personal relationships and the workplace. Similarly, acquiring knowledge in various disciplines can spark creativity by allowing you to make connections between seemingly unrelated topics. For instance, understanding basic psychology can enhance your appreciation of literature, while knowledge of technology can offer new insights into the arts. This holistic approach to learning makes the process more enjoyable and ensures that you are continually developing skills and insights that can be applied across various aspects of your life.

Lifelong Learning Resources

To support your continuous learning journey, numerous resources are available that cater to various interests and learning styles. Online platforms like Coursera and Udemy offer courses on everything from graphic design to philosophy, often taught by leading experts in the field. For those who prefer a more tactile learning experience, local workshops or seminars hosted by community centers or libraries provide opportunities to engage directly with subject-matter experts and fellow learners. Additionally, many universities now offer free or low-cost access to their course materials online, allowing you to explore academic subjects at your own pace. By taking advantage of these resources, you can construct a personalized learning plan that fits your interests and schedule, continually challenges you, and expands your horizons.

In weaving the threads of continuous learning into the fabric of your daily life, you enrich your mind and your emotional well-being. Each new piece of knowledge acquired acts as a stepping stone in the path of personal growth, leading you to a fuller, more satisfying life. As you turn the pages of this chapter, remember that pursuing knowledge is a lifelong journey that promises to keep your mind vibrant and your spirit engaged.

8.2 Harnessing Technology for Health: Apps and Tools

In the intricate dance of maintaining wellness in our digitally driven age, technology plays a dual role as both a facilitator and a potential source of stress. Recognizing how to utilize technology effectively for health enhancement without falling into the pitfalls of overuse is a skill that requires both awareness and discernment. Let's explore a curated selection of apps designed with your well-being in mind and discuss strategies to integrate these tools into your lifestyle in a balanced and secure manner.

Meditation apps like "Headspace" and "Calm" offer guided sessions that can help ground your day and manage stress. They provide various meditation scripts ranging from focus-building to relaxation techniques, making finding a meditation that resonates with your current needs easy. Fitness trackers, such as "Fitbit" or "Apple Watch," go beyond counting steps—they analyze sleep patterns, track heart rate variability, and can even offer personalized insights into your health trends. This data can help you make informed decisions about your physical activities and rest periods. Diet planners like "MyFitnessPal" or "Macros First" allow you to track your nutritional intake, ensuring you maintain a balanced diet that supports your energy levels and overall health.

While these apps offer numerous benefits, integrating them into your life without becoming overwhelmed requires setting clear boundaries. Start by identifying specific goals you wish to achieve with each tool: reducing stress, improving sleep, enhancing physical fitness, or monitoring dietary habits. Use these goals to guide you in selecting and configuring your apps to meet your needs effectively. For instance, if your aim is to enhance sleep quality, configure your fitness tracker to monitor sleep patterns and set reminders to wind down with a guided meditation before bed.

Balancing technology use is crucial to prevent the very tools designed to enhance your health from becoming sources of stress. It's easy to become preoccupied with the data and metrics these apps provide, leading to what's often called "analysis paralysis," where you're so caught up in tracking and optimizing every aspect of your health that it starts to dominate your life. To avoid this, set specific times to review your health metrics, perhaps once a week or biweekly instead of daily. This approach helps you gain benefits from the insights provided without becoming tethered to the constant feedback loop. Designate tech-free zones or times, such as during meals or in the bedroom, to help maintain a healthy balance between connectivity and relaxation.

Privacy and security considerations are paramount when using health and wellness apps. Personal data, such as health metrics and dietary habits, are sensitive and should be protected with the utmost caution. When choosing an app, research the developer's privacy policy to understand how your data will be used and protected. Look for apps that offer data encryption and do not share information with third parties without your consent. Moreover, regularly updating your apps and using strong, unique passwords for your accounts are basic but critical steps in protecting your personal information from unauthorized access.

By thoughtfully selecting and managing health-promoting technology, you empower yourself to harness the benefits of these tools effectively and safely. This proactive approach enhances your physical and mental well-being and ensures that your journey toward health remains both informed and secure. As you continue to explore and utilize these technological aids, remember that they are not just tools but partners in your ongoing quest for a healthier, more balanced life.

8.3 Building a Personal Wellness Plan

In the pursuit of a fulfilling life, creating a personal wellness plan stands as a cornerstone, not merely for preventing illness but for flourishing holistic health. This plan, unique to the individual it serves, encompasses a broad spectrum of health aspects, including physical, mental, and emotional dimensions. The initial step in crafting such a comprehensive plan involves a deep self-reflection on your current health status and lifestyle choices. Assess areas such as your physical activity levels, dietary habits, mental health state, and emotional well-being. This assessment will provide a clear starting point from which personalized goals can be set, guiding you toward a more balanced and healthy life.

Customization of your wellness plan is crucial and should align with your personal goals, lifestyle preferences, and health requirements. For instance, if you lead a hectic lifestyle, your plan might focus on integrating quick but effective stress-relief techniques and preparing simple, nutritious meals. If you have specific health conditions, such as diabetes or heart disease, your plan will include strategies and foods that address these issues. The key is to tailor the plan to improve your health and fit seamlessly into your daily routine, enhancing its sustainability and effectiveness.

Incorporating preventive health measures is another vital component of your wellness plan. Regular health screenings play a significant role in preventing diseases before they start or in catching them early when they are most treatable. Schedule regular check-ups with your healthcare provider to monitor key health metrics such as blood pressure, cholesterol levels, and other pertinent biomarkers. These preventive measures are an investment in your health capital, providing peace of mind and reducing potential healthcare costs in the future.

Regularly reviewing and adapting your wellness plan are essential to ensure its continued relevance and effectiveness. As your life circumstances change, so too should your wellness plan. This might involve adjusting your diet as you age, changing your physical activity levels based on your job demands or incorporating new stress-management techniques during particularly challenging periods. Regularly revisiting and tweaking your plan encourages a proactive approach to health management and keeps you aligned with your evolving health goals. For example, yearly reviews of your plan can be scheduled around significant dates like your birthday, making it a personal health ritual that ensures your wellness strategy remains aligned with your current needs and aspirations.

By thoughtfully creating and maintaining a personal wellness plan, you take an empowered step towards not just preventing disease but also enhancing your quality of life. This plan, reflective of your unique needs and goals, acts as a dynamic blueprint guiding you toward optimal health and well-being. As you implement and refine your plan, you'll discover that each choice and change, no matter how small, contributes significantly to a healthier, more vibrant you.

8.4 The Power of Gratitude and Positive Thinking

In the tapestry of life, the threads of gratitude and positive thinking are among the most vibrant, weaving patterns of resilience and contentment through the everyday fabric of our existence. Embracing an attitude of gratitude and maintaining a positive outlook are not merely passive states of mind but active processes that can significantly enhance both psychological and physical health. When you cultivate gratitude, you're acknowledging the good in your life and magnifying it, which can lead to a profound shift in the way you perceive and react to daily challenges.

The benefits of maintaining a gratitude-filled and optimistic mindset are well-documented. Psychologically, gratitude has been linked to increased levels of happiness and reduced depression. This is because focusing on positive elements can naturally reduce the space occupied by negative thoughts and worries. Physically, the practice of gratitude has been associated with better sleep, fewer headaches, and less illness; your body responds to positive mental states by reducing stress levels, which can improve overall health. Moreover, positive thinking helps forge a buffer against the common stressors of life, providing a psychological resilience that enables you to navigate difficulties with greater ease.

To integrate gratitude into your daily routine, one effective practice is gratitude journaling. This involves dedicating a few minutes each day to write down things you are thankful for. These can be as significant as family and friends or as simple as a cup of coffee that tasted wonderful. The key is consistency; by making this a regular practice, you train your mind to focus more on positive aspects, which can alter your overall perception and increase your mental well-being. Another enriching practice is gratitude visits, which involve writing a letter to someone who has made a positive impact on your life and expressing your appreciation. If possible, delivering this message in person can be incredibly impactful, both for you and the receiver. These practices enhance your well-being and strengthen your relationships by spreading positivity and appreciation.

Overcoming the brain's natural negativity bias — the tendency to pay more attention to negative experiences than positive ones — is another critical aspect of cultivating a positive mindset. The negativity bias is an evolutionary trait that helped our ancestors stay alert to threats, but in modern times, it can be less helpful, leading to stress and pessimism. To counteract this, make a conscious effort to recognize and savor positive moments throughout your day. This could be as simple as enjoying the warmth of the sun on your skin, savoring a delicious meal, or acknowledging a job well done. By intentionally focusing on these positive experiences, you can train your brain to notice and appreciate them more, which gradually diminishes the impact of negative biases.

The transformative power of gratitude and positive thinking is not just theoretical but is vividly illustrated in numerous testimonials and case studies. For instance, consider the story of Emma, a healthcare worker who started practicing gratitude journaling during a particularly stressful period. Over time, she noticed a significant decrease in her daily stress levels and an improvement in her relationships with colleagues and patients. Similarly, John, a school teacher, adopted the practice of starting each day by listing three things he was looking forward to. This simple ritual transformed his mornings, changing his outlook for the entire day from dread to anticipation. These stories underscore the profound impact that gratitude and positive thinking can have on individuals' mental health, their interactions, and overall quality of life.

By embracing the practices of gratitude and positive thinking, you open yourself to a life enhanced by greater joy, resilience, and health. Each positive thought and each moment of gratitude acts as a ripple, spreading out and touching every area of your life, infusing it with positivity. As you continue to cultivate these habits, watch as they become a natural part of your daily rhythm, enriching your experiences and interactions in deeply fulfilling ways.

8.5 Ongoing Mindfulness and Its Long-term Benefits

Deepening Mindfulness Practices

In your ongoing quest for wellness, adopting mindfulness as a regular practice is akin to nurturing a garden; it requires consistent care and attention but yields profound beauty and tranquility in return. Deepening your mindfulness practice isn't about allocating more hours of the day to seated meditation—it's about weaving mindfulness more intricately into the fabric of your daily life. One effective way to do this is through the practice of mindful awareness in routine activities. This could be as simple as being fully present while drinking your morning coffee, feeling the warmth of the cup in your hands, and truly tasting each sip, rather than mechanically drinking it while your mind wanders to the day's tasks. Similarly, transforming mundane activities like washing dishes or folding laundry into moments of mindfulness can turn them from chores into opportunities for calm and reflection.

Another method to deepen your mindfulness is through the integration of mindfulness reminders throughout your day. Use technology to your advantage by setting reminders on your phone or computer to pause, breathe, and center yourself for a minute or two. These brief pauses can serve as resets to a busy day, providing regular moments to ground yourself and gather your thoughts. Additionally, enrich your environment with cues that remind you to stay present. This could be a small post-it note on your monitor that says, "Breathe," or a picturesque calendar on your wall that invites a moment of peace whenever you glance at it. These small anchors can help maintain mindfulness throughout the day, making engaging with the practice consistently easier.

Long-term Benefits of Sustained Practice

The benefits of a sustained mindfulness practice are far-reaching, impacting various aspects of your life, from personal resilience to the quality of your relationships. Over time, regular mindfulness practice can enhance your ability to cope with stress by fostering a sense of ease and calmness in facing life's challenges. This cultivated resilience helps you recover from setbacks more quickly and equips you with the emotional flexibility to adapt to change and uncertainty with greater poise and less anxiety.

Emotionally, mindfulness helps regulate feelings and enhance self-awareness. By becoming more aware of your emotional patterns, you can better manage negative emotions such as anger or sadness and respond to situations with a more balanced and thoughtful approach. This emotional regulation is particularly beneficial in interpersonal relationships, where heightened self-awareness and empathy can lead to more meaningful and harmonious interactions. You might find that you are less reactive in stressful or challenging conversations, are able to listen more actively, and respond with greater understanding and less judgment.

Mindfulness Across Different Cultures and Practices

Exploring mindfulness through the lens of different cultural practices can enrich your understanding and appreciation of its versatility and universal relevance. For instance, in Japanese culture, the practice of Zen meditation emphasizes simplicity and concentration, offering a pathway to mindfulness through the cultivation of a clear, focused mind. In contrast, the Indian tradition of yoga incorporates mindfulness through physical postures and breathing exercises that align body and mind, promoting a harmonious balance. Engaging with these diverse practices broadens your perspective and allows you to discover the form of mindfulness that resonates most deeply with you, enriching your personal practice.

For those interested in integrating these varied cultural practices into their routines, local yoga classes, meditation centers, or even online courses can provide accessible gateways to learning. These resources often offer beginner-friendly sessions that introduce the fundamental aspects of different mindfulness practices, guided by experienced instructors who can provide insight and support as you explore new paths to mindfulness.

Overcoming Challenges in Sustaining Practice

Maintaining regular mindfulness practice amidst the demands of a busy life often presents challenges, primarily related to time constraints and waning motivation. To navigate these obstacles, consider mindfulness as an essential part of your daily routine rather than an optional activity. Just as you might schedule time for meals or exercise, reserve specific times in your day for mindfulness. Early morning, during lunch breaks, or before bedtime are all potential windows where you can incorporate a few minutes of mindful breathing or meditation.

Creating a dedicated mindfulness space in your home can also enhance your practice, making it more appealing and easier to commit to. This space doesn't need to be large—a corner of a room with a comfortable seat and perhaps a few calming elements like plants or soft lighting can make a significant difference. Moving to this dedicated space can help mentally shift gears towards calmness and focus, reinforcing your commitment to the practice.

Lastly, keep your practice dynamic by varying your mindfulness activities. If you find yourself losing interest in a particular meditation technique, experiment with other forms of mindfulness like guided imagery, progressive muscle relaxation, or even mindful walking. This variety can keep your practice engaging and prevent it from feeling like a routine chore.

By embracing mindfulness with a commitment to deepen and sustain your practice, you are setting a foundation for a life marked by greater peace, resilience, and emotional clarity. Each moment of mindfulness is a step towards a more centered and harmonious existence, enriching your life's journey with calm and purpose.

8.6 Setting Future Goals Without Overwhelming Yourself

Setting goals is akin to planting seeds in a garden in the landscape of personal and professional growth. You nurture them with your efforts and watch as they grow, pushing through the soil into the sunlight. However, unlike a garden where every seed is expected to sprout, it's essential to plant your goals wisely and tend to them in a way that ensures they flourish without overwhelming your resources. This careful cultivation involves setting realistic, achievable objectives that stretch your capabilities without straining them. For instance, if you're aiming to enhance your professional skills, setting a goal to learn a new, relevant skill every quarter can be more manageable and less stressful than aiming to master an entirely new domain in a short period.

Balancing ambition with personal well-being is crucial. It's easy to let professional aspirations consume all your energy, but true success is a blend of career achievement and personal satisfaction. Achieving this balance means setting goals that advance your career and enrich your personal life. For example, you might set a professional goal to lead a project at work while also setting a personal goal to spend at least two evenings per week unplugged with family or friends. This approach ensures that while you're pushing forward in your career, you're also nurturing your relationships and personal interests, which are essential for long-term happiness and resilience.

Goals should also serve as a source of motivation and inspiration, propelling you forward with a sense of purpose and excitement. To harness this positive power, setting goals aligned with your passions and values is important. When goals are connected to what truly matters to you, they naturally become more motivating. For instance, if you're passionate about environmental sustainability, setting a goal to implement green practices in your workplace can be incredibly fulfilling. This alignment ensures that your efforts feel meaningful and contribute to a greater sense of accomplishment and personal identity.

Regularly reviewing and adjusting your goals is essential to keep them aligned with your evolving priorities and life circumstances. Life is dynamic—changes in your personal environment, unexpected opportunities, or shifts in your interests can all impact the relevance of your goals. By taking time to reflect on your goals periodically—say, every three months—you can assess their progress, celebrate achievements, and make necessary adjustments. This might mean setting new goals, modifying existing ones, or even letting go of a goal if it no longer serves your best interests. Regular reviews keep your goals relevant and reinforce your commitment to them, keeping your motivation fresh and your approach flexible.

As we wrap up this section on setting goals without overwhelming yourself, remember that the key to effective goal-setting is not in the quantity but in the quality of the goals set. By focusing on realistic, balanced, and inspiring objectives and by regularly reviewing your progress, you can achieve a harmonious blend of personal and professional growth. This strategic approach advances your ambitions and enhances your overall well-being, ensuring that as you reach for the stars, you remain firmly grounded in what brings you joy and fulfillment. As you move forward, let these principles guide you in cultivating a life that feels as rewarding as it is successful, paving the way for sustained happiness and achievement.

Keeping the Wellness Alive

Now that you have everything you need to reduce stress, nurture your relationships, and improve your health and wellness, it's time to share what you've learned with others.

By leaving your honest opinion of this book on Amazon, you'll show other readers where they can find the help they need and share your passion for conquering burnout.

Thank you for your help. The fight against burnout is kept alive when we pass on our knowledge – and you're helping us to do just that.

Scan the QR code below to leave your review:

Conclusion

As we draw close to the end of our shared journey through understanding and overcoming burnout, let's take a moment to reflect on the crucial insights and strategies we've explored together. From recognizing the early signs of burnout through its debilitating stages to the empowering steps toward recovery, we have navigated a deeply personal and universally relevant path.

As we've learned, burnout is not merely a badge of overwork but a signal from our bodies and minds that something fundamental needs to change. We've delved into various recovery strategies—ranging from simple, immediate relief techniques to comprehensive lifestyle adjustments. These include psychological tools to manage stress, techniques for maintaining a healthy work-life balance, strategies for nurturing personal relationships, and essential practices for personal wellness.

It's important to remember that the journey to overcoming burnout is as individual as you are. The strategies and insights offered in this book are meant to be customized to fit your unique circumstances, challenges, and needs. There's no one-size-fits-all solution; what works wonderfully for one person might not be perfect for another. I encourage you to experiment with these tools, adapting and integrating them into your life in the most natural and beneficial ways.

Overcoming burnout is not a destination but a continuous journey of learning and self-discovery. It's about tuning in to your needs, recognizing your limits, and making intentional choices that align with your well-being. I urge you to keep exploring, keep learning, and keep growing. Each step you take is a step towards a more balanced and fulfilling life.

In this spirit, I cannot stress enough the importance of seeking support. Whether it's professional help, the comfort of peers, or the strength of a community, remember that reaching out is a sign of strength. It's okay not to have all the answers, and it's okay to need help. Building a support network can provide not only practical advice but also the emotional sustenance necessary for recovery.

Now, I invite you to take the first step, however small, towards your recovery and wellness. Perhaps choose one or two strategies from this book to implement this week. Each action, no matter the size, is a powerful signal to yourself that you are committed to your well-being.

As we conclude, I hold on to hope—not just for your recovery, but for your transformation. With the right tools and support, you can recover from burnout and thrive, leading a life that is not just about surviving but about flourishing.

Lastly, I invite you to share your journey with me. Your experiences, challenges, and successes in overcoming burnout can inspire and encourage others. We build a community of support, empathy, and empowerment by sharing our stories.

Thank you for allowing me to be a part of your journey. Here's to a balanced, vibrant, and fulfilling life ahead.

References

Stanton, J. (2020, November 23). *The surprising difference between stress and burnout.* Psychology Today. https://www.psychologytoday.com/us/blog/the-right-mindset/202011/the-surprising-difference-between-stress-and-burnout

StatPearls. (n.d.). *Physiology, cortisol.* In *StatPearls.* StatPearls Publishing. Retrieved July 25, 2024, from https://www.ncbi.nlm.nih.gov/books/NBK538239/#:

Pines, A., & Maslach, C. (2020). *Burnout assessment tool (BAT)—Development, validity, and reliability.* NCBI Bookshelf. https://www.ncbi.nlm.nih.gov/pmc/articles/PMC7766078/

Brough, P., & O'Driscoll, M. P. (2023). *Is gender an antecedent to workplace stressors? A systematic review.* NCBI Bookshelf. https://www.ncbi.nlm.nih.gov/pmc/articles/PMC10139098/

HelpGuide. (n.d.). *Stress management: Techniques & strategies to deal with stress.* HelpGuide. Retrieved July 25, 2024, from https://www.helpguide.org/articles/stress/stress-management.htm

RescueTime. (2023, May 16). *How to recover from burnout: 5 survivors share their stories, struggles, and strategies.* RescueTime. https://blog.rescuetime.com/how-to-recover-from-burnout/

Sarris, J., & Kahn, R. (2018). *Food, mood, and brain health: Implications for the modern diet.* NCBI Bookshelf. https://www.ncbi.nlm.nih.gov/pmc/articles/PMC6170050/

Mayo Clinic. (n.d.). *Exercise and stress: Get moving to manage stress.* Mayo Clinic. Retrieved July 25, 2024, from https://www.mayoclinic.org/healthy-lifestyle/stress-management/in-depth/exercise-and-stress/art-2004446

Mayo Clinic. (n.d.). *Mindfulness exercises.* Mayo Clinic. Retrieved July 25, 2024, from https://www.mayoclinic.org/healthy-lifestyle/consumer-health/in-depth/mindfulness-exercises/art-20046356

Gaiam. (2023, July 11). *Meditation 101: Techniques, benefits, and a beginner's how-to.* Gaiam. https://www.gaiam.com/blogs/discover/meditation-101-techniques-benefits-and-a-beginner-s-how-to

NHS. (n.d.). *Online self-help CBT techniques.* Every Mind Matters. Retrieved

July 25, 2024, from https://www.nhs.uk/every-mind-matters/mental-wellbeing-tips/self-help-cbt-techniques/

Positive Psychology. (n.d.). *13 emotional intelligence activities, exercises & PDFs.* Retrieved July 25, 2024, from https://positivepsychology.com/emotional-intelligence-exercises/

Clockify. (n.d.). *26 most effective time management techniques.* Retrieved July 25, 2024, from https://clockify.me/time-management-techniques

AMFM. (n.d.). *Work life balance and mental health: Importance.* AMFM Treatment. Retrieved July 25, 2024, from https://amfmtreatment.com/work-life-balance-and-mental-health/

Bendau, A., Plag, J., & Kocalevent, R. D. (2023). *Remote work burnout, professional job stress, and employee turnover intentions during the COVID-19 pandemic. NCBI Bookshelf.* https://www.ncbi.nlm.nih.gov/pmc/articles/PMC10267312/#:

Crucial Learning. (2023, May 2). *Crucial applications: How to negotiate workload limits.* Crucial Learning. https://cruciallearning.com/blog/crucial-applications-how-to-negotiate-workload-limits/

Positive Psychology. (n.d.). *7 ways to improve communication in relationships.* Retrieved July 25, 2024, from https://positivepsychology.com/communication-in-relationships/

Choi, M., & Kim, J. (2024). *Social support and mental health: The mediating role of coping strategies. NCBI Bookshelf.* https://www.ncbi.nlm.nih.gov/pmc/articles/PMC10915202/

Healthline. (2023, January 12). *Burnout recovery: 11 strategies to help you reset.* Healthline. https://www.healthline.com/health/mental-health/burnout-recovery

Smith, M. (2023, August 3). *Family conflict resolution tips and strategies.* Verywell Mind. https://www.verywellmind.com/family-conflict-resolution-solutions-3144540

American Psychological Association. (2013, March 6). *Stress and sleep.* American Psychological Association. https://www.apa.org/news/press/releases/stress/2013/sleep

Harvard Health Publishing. (2015, November 16). *Nutritional psychiatry: Your brain on food.* Harvard Health Blog. https://www.health.harvard.edu/blog/nutritional-psychiatry-your-brain-on-food-201511168626

Huang, C. Y., & Shih, H. T. (2020). *How leisure activities affect health: A narrative review and meta-analysis. NCBI Bookshelf.* https://www.ncbi.nlm.nih.gov/pmc/articles/PMC7613155/

Maurer, T. (2023, August 6). *Taking the stress out of financial planning.* Forbes.

https://www.forbes.com/sites/timmaurer/2023/08/06/taking-the-stress-out-of-financial-planning/

Sogolow, E. D., & Kahn, C. H. (2024). *Strategies and interventions to improve healthcare worker mental health: A systematic review. NCBI Bookshelf.* https://www.ncbi.nlm.nih.gov/pmc/articles/PMC10233581/

Morin, A. (2023, May 9). *11 effective ways to cope with entrepreneurial stress.* Entrepreneur. https://www.entrepreneur.com/leadership/11-effective-ways-to-cope-with-entrepreneurial-stress/412401

Child Mind Institute. (n.d.). *Why self-care is essential to parenting.* Retrieved July 25, 2024, from https://childmind.org/article/fighting-caregiver-burnout-special-needs-kids/

Harvard Medical School. (n.d.). *Stress management and resiliency training (SMART).* Harvard Medical School. Retrieved July 25, 2024, from https://cmecatalog.hms.harvard.edu/stress-management-and-resiliency-training-smart-program

Transformations Network. (2023, June 15). *How lifelong learning benefits your mental health.* Transformations Network. https://www.transformationsnetwork.com/post/how-lifelong-learning-benefits-your-mental-health

Tipalti. (2023, February 22). *Best wellness apps in 2023.* Tipalti. https://tipalti.com/guide/best-wellness-apps-2023/

Scripps AMG. (n.d.). *Creating your personal wellness plan.* Scripps AMG. Retrieved July 25, 2024, from https://scrippsamg.com/personal-wellness-plan/

Emmons, R. A. (2020, November 23). *How gratitude changes you and your brain.* Greater Good Science Center. https://greatergood.berkeley.edu/article/item/how_gratitude_changes_you_and_your_brain

Made in the USA
Coppell, TX
20 November 2024

40615742R00089